JAPAN'S INFORMATION WAR

NANCY SNOW

About the Author

Nancy Snow (Ph.D., International Relations) is Pax Mundi Professor of Public Diplomacy at Kyoto University of Foreign Studies. She is the first professor in Japan with the academic title of public diplomacy. Snow is also Adjunct Fellow in the Institute of Contemporary Asian Studies (ICAS) at Temple University Japan.

From 2013-2015 Snow was a Visiting Professor and Abe Fellow at Keio University's Institute for Media and Communications Research. She is a two-time Fulbright scholar (Germany, Japan) and has published ten other books, including *Information War, Propaganda, Inc., Propaganda and American Democracy, Routledge Handbook of Public Diplomacy and The Routledge Handbook of Critical Public Relations*. Her books have been translated into Arabic, Chinese, Farsi, Japanese, Korean and Portuguese.

Two flagship American universities recruited Snow to serve as an expert leader in public diplomacy. She was hired as faculty consultant to establish the University of Southern California Center on Public Diplomacy where she became its first Senior Research Fellow. She taught the first public diplomacy course on international exchanges in USC's Master of Public Diplomacy program and published the first edited volume on public diplomacy with leading British scholar Philip M. Taylor. Syracuse University recruited her to be the first titled public diplomacy professor in the dual degree masters sponsored by the Maxwell School of Citizenship and Public Affairs and the S.I. Newhouse School of Public Communications. In 2014 she retired early as Full Professor in the College of Communications at California State University, Fullerton and was appointed Professor Emeritus of Communications in 2015.

Snow teaches public diplomacy and nation branding as a visiting professor at Tsinghua University in Beijing, China. She has been a visiting professor in public diplomacy at the IDC Herzliya's Lauder School of Government, Diplomacy and Strategy in Israel and Universiti Teknologi MARA (UiTM) Centre for Media and Information Warfare Studies in Shah Alam, Malaysia. Her writing has appeared widely, including the *Los Angeles Times, New York*

Times, Newsday, Washington Post, Japan Times, and *The Huffington Post.*

In addition to her academic work, Snow serves as advisor in public affairs, leadership, and media relations at Langley Esquire in Tokyo, Japan. She is global strategy director at La Ditta Limited, a boutique firm that specializes in promoting Japanese products and services overseas.

For more information, visit http://www.nancysnow.com or follow her on Twitter (@drpersuasion).

TO THE JAPANESE PEOPLE,
JAPAN'S GREATEST PUBLIC RESOURCE
TO THE WORLD

If you understand everything, you must be misinformed.

Japanese Proverb

I never chose Japan. Japan chose me.

I was chosen to come to Japan over two decades ago at the invitation of the Prime Minister's Office.[1] It's an accident of being in the right place at the right time. I walked into an office about one piece of business unrelated to Japan and walked out of it ready to pack my bags for destination unknown. It wasn't my idea to go, but if someone were going to offer me a free trip to a faraway, exotic destination, and a chance to be out of my federal government office cubicle for three weeks in July, then sign me up! (I never knew that the hot and humid summers in Washington, DC were so comparable to Tokyo summers.)

For those of us who are global sojourners, there are countries that do the choosing and there are countries that we choose. Most of the time we decide where to go. We want to be aware of the seasonal climate conditions, the safety and security statistics, what we'll study or what sites we'll see from our bucket list, what cuisine we will encounter, and where we'll stay–from youth hostel to the fanciest 5-star hotel. But mostly we want to know how well we can communicate our wants and needs to our hosts. One global nomad friend, Carole Rosenblatt, has an entirely different approach. She invites anyone to vote where she will travel next in the world. "Drop Me Anywhere"[2] is her travel blog name, which puts the wheel of fortune (or misfortune) in the hands of Internet friends and acquaintances. How many of us would have the courage to do that? One time I checked, the voters were kind enough to choose Bali as her next destination and her Instagram posts were full of palm trees, temples, and drinks with umbrellas.

Japan was one place on the global map that I never sought out or wished that I could be dropped. I was defined by and attached to my regional locale. I grew up in the Southeast of the United States and strongly identify with a subregion known as the Deep South, home to my birthplace in Augusta, Georgia and the birthplace of my father's side of the family in the Tuscaloosa and Birmingham area of Alabama. My geological frame of reference, outside of a six-year stint in Michigan when I was a child, tended to stretch from Georgia to Washington, D.C.

Until I was twenty years old I had never traveled outside the United States. I was the only daughter to grateful parents, especially my mother, who lost her own mother shortly after she was born. As a sister to four older brothers, this family dynamic led to a lot of teasing by my brothers as a bit "spoiled" and overprotected by a mother who had once been convinced that she could only produce boys. One of my brothers earned my lifelong appreciation for showing off his baby sister in his school's "Show and Tell" sharing time. My father let me do whatever I wanted, and were he alive today would be very supportive of my wanderlust.

At 20, I took the predictable overseas path. I went to Europe with a couple of my German professors and a small group of students from Clemson University, a national public university in Clemson, South Carolina.[3] According to the U.S. Department of Commerce's National Travel and Tourism Office, with the exception of nearby and drivable North American neighboring countries of Mexico and Canada, Europe is still the most popular overseas destination for American tourists, comprising almost twenty percent of the market share, followed by the Caribbean with ten percent. The Asian continent, with seven percent of the American tourist share, may seem too far in distance and too culturally and linguistically different to garner more visits. When I had the chance to return to Europe as a Fulbright scholar, the obvious destination was the Federal Republic of Germany, my maternal ancestral heritage. German was a foreign language I had studied since high school, and so I was comfortable with the thought of living there for a year to expand my German knowledge and language facility.

Asia was always the furthest thought from my mind. I hadn't taken one class in Asian politics or culture at the undergraduate level or even graduate school, despite my earning a doctorate in international relations. Many of my doctoral courses at American University's School of International Service in Washington, D.C. focused on the US/USSR relationship of the Cold War, which, unbeknownst to our professors and us know-it-alls, was about to end.

Whenever I thought about Asia, it was about its economic and cultural might, such as my Sony Walkman or Japanese-made car. Japan seemed a place that made functional things that people around the world wanted to use. From a distance and as a consumer, Japan was user-friendly. I wasn't caught up in any Japan bashing vis-à-vis its trade protectionism, nor was I easily swayed by the "Japan that can say no" prognostications of Sony's Akio Morita and the LDP's Shintaro Ishihara, which predicted that Japan would overtake the United States as the next economic superpower.

The other Asian place I thought about peripherally was Vietnam, a remote jungle-looking place that was delivered to my family room each week in the form of full color bloody pictures on the cover of *Look* and *Life* magazines. As a young child my thoughts toward Vietnam were mostly relief and a fuzzy recollection of my mother's tears at hearing the good news that her two oldest sons would be spared the possibility of returning home in body bags from Southeast Asia.[4] It was almost as if CBS News had reported it directly: "Suzanne Snow's sons have avoided by sheer luck the bloody hell of Vietnam, which will only end in stalemate and no victory. This is Walter Cronkite. Good night."

So how did I find myself in Japan eighteen years after the end of the Vietnam War and just months after my doctoral hooding? I was working as a Presidential Management Fellow at the United States Information Agency in Washington, D.C.[5] The PMF Program is a federal management fast track to upper level positions in the executive branch in the U.S. government. Many of us jump ship after the two mandatory years of the program—government work isn't everyone's idea of a dream job–but I was just nine months into my tenure and wasn't thinking about going anywhere. I stopped by the Youth Programs Division to get a signature for an academic exchange program. I was not there for anything related to Japan, but my co-worker overseeing a youth exchange program asked me a question that would change my life. "How would you like to go to Japan this summer, Nancy?" This is what led to my participation in the International Youth Village '93, which was administered by the Prime Minister's Office.[6]

My first encounter with Japan, outside of the extremely long but pleasant on-board experience with Japan Airlines (JAL), left an indelible impression on how the government of Japan approached sharing information. I'll never forget our being led from Narita International Airport to the awaiting limousine bus and to the Park Hyatt Tokyo in the bustling Shinjuku district. While on the bus, two lady guides handed out a list of do's and don'ts regarding how to comport ourselves in this most special country—Japan. I have no doubt that their actions were well intended: they did not want newcomers to violate cultural norms and thereby cause embarrassment on our—or our hosts'—part. But the message I got was that I had to adapt swiftly to my host culture because it was I who had more to learn about Japan from the Japanese than I could teach them as an American citizen and U.S. government official. Japan's information exchange seemed a bit one-way, but when intercultural communication is perceived as such, it often makes the receiver feel inadequate. I felt I would have to walk on cultural eggshells to maneuver my Japanese environment.

I returned to Tokyo for a two-week stay one year later as delegation leader for the Japan-America Leadership Exchange Committee (JALEC). My chance meeting at USIA had led to two impressive professional exchanges, but I wasn't yet wedded to Japan. You might call the relationship one of cordial acquaintances.

A full decade and a half would pass before I would return to Nippon. In the meantime, my first two books, *Propaganda, Inc.* and *Information War*, were translated into Japanese. I marveled at the gorgeous design covers with the Kanji, Hiragana and Katakana artistry, but being a published author in Japan wasn't enough to give me a sense of longing to return. Once again, it was a serendipitous pull factor from inside Japan that led to my return in 2010. The U.S. Embassy in Tokyo sought me out as an American expert on public diplomacy. I was asked to participate in a U.S. Speaker Program[7] sponsored by the U.S. Department of State to explain the public diplomacy of President Barack Obama's administration.

The issues I discussed with my Japanese audiences included Obama's outreach to Muslim communities in the Middle East, the change of rhetoric and practice in the Obama administration's approach to terrorism, and the strong emphasis on social media, social networking and Internet freedom under Secretary of State Hillary Clinton. I spoke in Okinawa, Fukuoka, Nagoya, Osaka and Tokyo. Despite my long absence from Japan, I became convinced during my encounters with many Japanese that the U.S.-Japan relationship was our most important bilateral relationship in the East Asia region and that Japan had much to share with the United States about cultural diplomacy, international exchange and visitor hospitality.

Nowadays I choose to live in Japan, which is why I wrote this book: to explain the enigma of Japanese information power, to paraphrase my friend, Karel van Wolferen. Why associate it with war? War is my metaphor for the battle of narratives and storytelling about Japan and its relationship with the world.

I believe Japan is one of the most fascinating countries on the planet that needs more communication sharing, exchange, and influence in the world. It also needs internal optimism about the world outside, outsider encouragement about its own storytelling, and more *Yoyu* (elbowroom) in which to take risks and think beyond *Kuru* Cool Japan, *Kawaii* cute culture or Abenomics. Japan is too important of a partner and leader in this world not to have reached a level of international communication that it should. Further, Japan is more than its government and political economy. Not enough stories from everyday people are being shared. Too many stories from the top down are being delegated. Those cultural eggshells that I used to walk on have now transferred increasingly to the Japanese people, who strike me at times as a bit powerless to change the national narrative that is being directed from the power centers at the top.

The place that we call Japan is quite simply a geographical marvel. An archipelago of 6,852 islands, just over four hundred are inhabited and four are dominant: Hokkaido, Honshu, Shikoku, and Kyushu. The best known and largest is Honshu, home to Tokyo, Yokohama, Osaka, Nagoya, Kobe, and Kyoto. Most stories in and out of Japan originate in Honshu, and even more specifically, Tokyo. This too is where I live.

Tokyo is the gold standard of soft power among megacities. It fascinates and illuminates the imagination of what a global city should offer—outstanding cuisine that equals or surpasses the best that Paris has to offer, public transportation that safely and efficiently delivers over forty million daily passengers through the world's largest urban rail system, and a hybrid mix of popular and traditional culture around every turn. Tokyo's heartbeat exists in the imagination of any tech geek or cosplayer,[8] which is not to say that you should expect everyone to be crowded in the city's electronic district of Akihabara or sashaying with whiskers and cat ears down Harajuku's Takeshita-dori. Tokyoites do go about their daily business just like other large urban populations. The media tendency is to highlight the extremes that Tokyo has to offer, but living here, I see how normal and predictable big city life can be.

Japan is a country of 126 million in one of the most geopolitically tense and economically rich areas of the world—Northeast Asia. It sits gingerly next to its ex-occupied territory of thirty-five years, South Korea, a country with less than half the population of Japan at 50 million, but with an economic growth trajectory known as Miracle on the Han River that rivals Japan. Japan was the East Asian country we associated with the post-war economic miracle. When Japan's economy began to take off in the 1960s, Korea was still ranked among the world's poorest nations. Today the Republic of Korea is among the wealthiest market economies and its popular culture, known as the Korean Wave or *Hallyu*, is not just a global phenomenon but also increasingly popular in Japan, a country known for its Western popular culture enthusiasm. Middle-aged Japanese women have become accidental cultural mediators between Japan and Korea. As Japanese scholar Atsushi Takeda explains: "Their admiration for Korean dramas as well as the country's actors is further extended to a positive image of Korean men. Middle-aged Japanese women have created non-political, grassroots connections with Korea that politics and economics could not fully achieve."[9]

Korea sits sandwiched between two of the top three economies in the world. As *The Economist* notes, "Before the wars of the 20th century Korea was a bridge between the more closed worlds of China and Japan."[10] On a recent trip to Seoul, I suggested that Korea act as a "people's diplomacy" bridge between China and Japan in the 21st century.

China and Japan reside as economically and nationalistically competitive neighbors that Robert Frost would say are in need of good fences. Both are major soft power projectors in the world, one more overtly in search of credibility and connection (China), and the other less assertive in its global outreach initiatives while resting on its cultural laurels and an uptick in foreign tourists (Japan). One country, China, still connotes expansion; the other, Japan, connotes shrinkage. Japan's population of 126 million is estimated to shrink by 30 million by 2050, while China's population of 1.36 billion will likely grow slightly or level off but age similarly as Japan. China lapped Japan's economy in 2010, another nail in the economic coffin known as Japan, Inc.[11]

Although Japan, Inc. is no more, Japan is still a global economic powerhouse. Where it diminishes itself is in the area of information and strategic narrative. Japan remains in the world but not fully communicating with it. It is a powerful nation-state but not necessarily the global communication power it could or should be. In my experience, Japan struggles with internationalization and international communication. We could call it a condition of Mundi Mendonication, a portmanteau of Mundi, the Latin word for world plus the Japanese word "Mendo," meaning difficulty or annoyance. This refers to Japan's being a product of its own isolated history that kept it on its own path, where it didn't have to make adjustment to communicating too often with other persons. It also refers to a pride in doing things a certain way and worrying that too much foreign intervention will dilute the Japanese identity. In Japan, going global is both difficult and annoying at times. It is Mundi Mendonication, which cannot be fixed entirely by Nomunication, the other more familiar portmanteau (at least in Japan) that combines the Japanese word "Nomu" (to drink) with communication. In the United States, our own form of Nomunication is called Liquid Courage.

In the pages that follow, I make a case for Japan to declare independence from too much inward-lookingness, become a global player in peace and sustainable development, and not slink away from the globalization that will see English as the most popular second language spoken, more foreign visitors inside its borders, and more global ways of doing things that are not always "The Japan Way." This is a proud nation, and so I do not expect changes to happen fast, but some will come, like it or not, while other changes will slowly impact Japan, and for the best. This is my love letter to a place I now call my second home.

Nancy Snow
July 2016

TABLE OF CONTENTS

PREFACE

This collection is about the challenges that Japan has in its global communication outreach and how this impacts Japan's soft power efforts to inform, engage and influence global publics in support of Japan's policies and values. It's called *Japan's Information War* to connote a state of flux, fight, and competition. War has several meanings. We know it primarily as a period of fighting between countries, but it is also an ongoing situation in which people in groups compete with and fight against each other. It can also mean an organized effort by a government or other large organization to stop or defeat something that is viewed as dangerous or bad, i.e., war on terrorism, war on drugs, as we declare in the United States. Japan has an ongoing war with information—image, reputation, narrative, who Japan is, where it is going. There are many players involved in this information war from the top echelons of government, within industry, and among the grassroots protesters in the streets.

During most of my writing time for this book, I was living part-time in Tokyo, Japan as an Abe Fellow and Visiting Professor at Keio University's Institute of Media and Communications Research. My 12-month Abe fellowship from the Social Science Research Council was a full-time research fellowship with no teaching commitments. There was no better time to do my study on Japan's global public diplomacy initiatives. My grant period covered the announcement of the Tokyo 2020 Summer Olympics to Abe's push for Womenomics, to Abe's return to power with a stronger emphasis on Brand Abe and Brand Japan. It included bumps along the path toward global information engagement: islands in dispute, official visits to Yasukuni shrine, 70th anniversary WWII statements, state secrets laws, media criticism and monitoring, and collective security decisions that challenged Japan's pacifist stance.

In my two years of research, I spent hundreds of hours in conversation with Japan culture and communication experts, Japanese business people, and Japanese and foreign academics who know Japan better than I do and for a lot longer. They schooled me well. In turn, I was asked then, as I'm continually asked now, to brief government, academic and private sector Japanese who are tackling the challenges and opportunities of nation brand Japan's going global. Whether speaking to a high-level ministry official or a university student, I always tell them that my expertise is derived from the intersection between Japan and the world. I'm not a speaker of Japanese outside of my limited getting around vocabulary (a deficit condition I plan to overcome), nor am I a specialist about traditional Japanese culture or modern Japanese popular culture. My contribution to Japan is as a global citizen and educator with a simple goal: to help Japan better understand how to engage effectively with the world and for the world to better engage with Japan. In addition, I am approaching this subject as a global communicator who has over twenty years of nation branding experience, including that "other" superpower that is a leading political, economic, military, and cultural fixture in the world. Now that I spend more time outside the United States, I'm able to look at other countries—not just Japan—with fresh eyes and a curious mind. I'm not trying to be right or necessarily authoritative as much as a contributor to an ongoing communication (perhaps over drinks!) that extends beyond the dimensions of this book.

Think of this book as a dialogue starter over definitive guide.

To begin, I'm an optimistic realist. I believe that a significant number of the Japanese people have made the choice for global engagement, and now they just need more confidence in global communication exchange, the kind that gets them beyond narrow politics and contested historical narratives. Japan's global voice is too top-down and not far and wide. I hope to change that. The way I approach it is to keep encouraging Japanese people to share their stories with the world, a leftover mandate from my days working at the U.S. Information Agency during Bill Clinton's first term as president.

My main thesis is that Japan is operating on a half tank of enthusiasm and strategy in its international relations. The Japan I know is one that often displays an enigmatic attitude toward anything that originates outside Japan. On the one hand, Japan wants to open itself up more, and even is opening itself up now, through advocating for more English use, globalization of universities, Cool Japan promotional campaigns, Japan House cultural community centers in global capitals, and even an embrace of foreign workers with special skills that are in demand. It is also remaking itself as a so-called 'normal' nation that can use its military offensively and cooperatively with allies like the United States. On the other hand, the Japan global communication embrace is always somewhat stiff and unnatural, as if the world is the aunt or uncle you see once a year with whom you really don't know how to engage in comfortable conversation.

In the back of the Japanese mind there is still a sense of threat and a question, "What are we giving up in exchange for such a global embrace?" The worry is that Japan will no longer be Japan.

The problem with worrying about Japan of yesterday is that you cannot relive history. You may be able to acknowledge history or even apologize about history, but you can never go back to what was, or what you think it was. You only have now, not the Edo, Heian, Tokugawa or Meiji period, however much they educate and inform. And now is the time for Japan to be a global national leader. I'm not one who is in favor of changing Japan's national security profile to one that will allow it to engage in international arms trade or international military interventions. Remember, I'm from the United States, and we have paid dearly in blood, money, and reputation since 9/11. But if a more US-emulative Japan is the one we are going to have, then there is no better time for Japan to accept its global reputation responsibility that comes with lethal force intervention.

In the pages that follow I will share a critique of Japan's slow roll toward global communication, but for the most part I will argue that Japan doesn't yet fully recognize what gifts it already has. Too often its story to the world is one of panic or alarm at an aging and declining population and dying rural communities. It must open itself up more, as Rakuten's Hiroshi Mikitani and others advocate, not just because it's good for business and will help to grow Japan's economy, but because the world needs lessons from Japan about how to do more with less—its primary national narrative—within the context of a spirit of excellence and good manners.

Japan has been described often as nice, and it is. That's why I live and work here, but nice isn't all that the government of Japan wants to be in a world that doesn't have all the public niceties. I would prefer that Japan's government embrace the world as a peace partner and use its unique platform of having been the only nation that has suffered the ravages of two atomic bombs in service to humanity. For a country that brands itself so often as unique, Article 9 is one of the unique features of its constitution to share with the world. Maintaining a renunciation of war stance while establishing a global leader in technology, hospitality, and sustainability in the face of a shrinking population, limited natural resources and a shaky natural foundation, has led to a population of survivors who persevere and rebuild themselves, all to the wonder of the world. The stories of the Japanese as Survivors and Thrivers, who created one of the world's most advanced economies, is a story that is yet to be fully shared with the world. I hope that this book will help Japan tell its story better, prouder and even louder, although not so loud that it would disturb the neighbors!

INTRODUCTION

On July 2, 2015, the multi-billionaire CEO of Rakuten, Hiroshi Mikitani, posted two short blogs of under 400 words each on his LinkedIn Influencer page. The first, "Japan is Going English,"[12] was very simple in message, but nevertheless popular. (I have a theory that we tend to listen more to billionaires.) Mikitani boasted that Rakuten is engaged in global recruiting because of its English adoption, "attracting graduates of the best foreign universities such as Harvard, Yale, Stanford, Cambridge, Peking University and the Indian Institute of Technology." The implication was that traditional Japanese companies that use Japanese or require foreign talent to use Japanese in their day-to-day operations are missing out on this global competition for the best and brightest. He compared Japan to the rest of Asia, not in a particularly positive light, but with a hope for change:

> I believe Singapore is so successful because English is one of its official languages. It is a strategy that allows it to attract and employ the best workers from all over the world. I believe if Japan were to make English one of its official languages, it would make Japan a real economic powerhouse, creating a powerful edge over China and South Korea.[13]

That's a big IF from Mikitani, because I believe Japan is one of the least likely countries to make English one of its official languages. Until and unless the Japanese educational system fully embraces English and at an early childhood education level, the Japanese will remain largely ill prepared to place English on par with Japanese. Many of my Japanese students tell me that the way they were taught English in primary and secondary school was Mendo-style, difficult, annoying, anything but pleasant and fun. English is still seen as too much of an invasion threat or some kind of dilution of Japanese. But isn't it possible to be supportive of one's native language and add another? Yes, just ask a Chinese, Korean, Taiwanese or the more than one and a half billion people studying English as their second language. As one native Japanese public relations expert told me, "Although we should protect our own language and culture, we should leverage English as communications tools more commonly, not as a special tool."[14]

The second Mikitani blog on July 8, 2015, "Japan Needs to Think Like a Global Citizen,"[15] continued the topic about Japan's difficult communication in both English and in engaging the world. In it, Mikitani referred to his first blog that called for mandatory global business English:

Last week I stirred controversy when writing about how Japan is going English. I wrote that Rakuten's 'Englishnization' has helped us grow as a global company by attracting the best talent from around the world and by making global business easier. Now several global Japanese companies are following suit. I believe Japan needs to think like a global citizen. In many ways, today, that's not the case.

It's hard to fathom that a declaration that Japan should utilize more English in global business is necessarily controversial these days. One of Japan's iconic automobile brands, Honda, announced in its Honda Sustainability Report 2015 that it was going to set English as the official language in its interregional communication as well as strengthen its global communication.[16] Nevertheless, the policy change made worldwide headlines to strengthen Mikitani's point that embracing English is still seen as a bit 'un-Japanese,' even as it was for decades at a global car company like Honda. As a devoted Honda driver and member of the 200k Club (214,000+ miles and counting on my 1998 Honda Civic), I was particularly happy to see Honda take the lead for other Japanese companies to follow.

The controversy in the first blog wasn't so much in what Mikitani had to say. The controversy was more about his target audience. He was speaking directly to the Japanese people about Japan's future and what was holding it back. If Mikitani had been directing his remarks about embracing English or globalization to a Korean or Chinese audience, he would have been deemed a bit bizarre since Korea and China already fully embrace a both/and model of international communication that combines the native with English as a secondary language. But Japan struggles with its global identity and has not yet become a citizen of the world. It does not think like a global citizen, Mikitani says, because of Japan's history and culture, using a highly difficult language and an ocean as a buffer against the world. Japanese, Chinese, Korean, and Arabic are the Department of State-designated "Superhard Languages," considered "exceptionally difficult" for native English speakers. They require up to two years of full-time study for diplomats before placement in the respective host country.[17]

Mikitani explained Japan's historical isolation of two hundred years as responsible for development of a "unique culture and civilization in the midst of a changing world."[18] That's pretty well documented, but to add a bit more context, Japan has played off this 'unique culture and civilization' reputation of being unlike anything or anywhere else on the planet since the Tokugawa or Edo period (1603-1867). I'm no Japanese historian, but the Tokugawa period comes up in conversation quite a bit in Japan as a historical precedent for Japan's fickleness today about globalization. It's been described as a period of "peace, political stability, and economic growth under the shogunate (military dictatorship) founded by Tokugawa Ieyasu."[19] In exchange for this stability, "the social order was officially frozen, and mobility between the four classes (i.e., warriors, farmers, artisans, and merchants) was prohibited. Numerous members of the warrior class, or samurai, took up residence in the capital and other castle towns where many of them became bureaucrats. Peasants, who made up 80 percent of the population, were forbidden to engage in non-agricultural activities so as to insure a stable and continuing source of income for those in positions of authority. Another aspect of the Tokugawa concern with political stability was fear of foreign ideas and military intervention."[20] There you have it. Perhaps historical DNA has a part to play in preventing global thinking today. But we shouldn't overplay that card.

An obvious card to play in one's global deck is history. Japan has not come to terms with its loss in World War Two. Just as the United

States still suffers the residual effects of Vietnam, which is not even close to the scale of World War II, Japan's complete defeat in 1945 left it with two minds toward the world. It embraced the postwar world largely through economics and through becoming a leading peaceful nation directing humanitarian aid and know-how to developing countries. But it surely must still sting for a prideful nation to live with a modern war history that has not been examined in full. Without such full examination and revelation of documents of record, I do not see Japan fully sharing itself with the world.

You could say that the early to mid-20th century Japan was then and that this is now. But maybe then is still now in the sense that fear, humiliation, and insecurity are driving factors in the Japanese mindset toward globalization. We who live in Tokyo and other large cities see (and mostly hear) the public presence of far right conservative nationalists who want to preserve pre-war Japan in the present. So it is not just Japan's information war with the world at stake here. It is as much about Japan's internal battles with its image, a national pride struggle between political leaders and the people.

Mikitani's blog about global citizenship compares the Japanese to Americans and Europeans. He describes Westerners as adventurers who travel the world frequently, but most especially, look at the world as a target marketplace for ideas and products. In contrast, Mikitani describes the Japanese as a people who go outside Japan to the world for a 'venture' but they almost always return. (I would add that the Japanese are probably returning for the high quality cuisine, some of the best in the world, but Mikitani did not mention Japanese food as a pull factor.) The Japanese national psyche toward the world is more about taking small steps toward globalization. Globalization, it seems, is always something to be most cautious about because of its potential deleterious effect on Japan's unique culture.

The bottom line is that it does not come as natural for the Japanese to feel at one with the world or connected to the world. The persistent mentality is more about Japan versus the world instead of Japan in the world. An either/or stance breeds feelings of defensiveness and insecurity, whereas a sense of belonging breeds confidence and enthusiasm for new challenges.

Mikitani ends his blog with a call to arms to embrace the world: "Unless we do away with this sentiment, we will not be able to adapt when the Internet finally does erase national boundaries. We will be manipulated by the people, capital, and information coming like a giant wave into Japan, and we will lose sight of the path that our nation must follow."

His use of the word 'manipulation' was quite telling. It's a warning to the Japanese government, business, and society that Japan is having its proverbial tail kicked by the world, a world of nations unafraid by internationalization. Even the most reviled rogue wannabe nation-state known as the Islamic State (IS, ISIL or ISIS) is more globally nimble. These nation-states and non-state terrorists maneuver borders better than Japan. In the case of ISIS, using English, Twitter, and global public relations strategies and tactics recruits more sacrificial soldiers in the march toward a global Islamic caliphate. Whatever the goal—noble or militant, global actors continue to lap Japan around the communications track.

Japan's efforts to communicate with the world are made even more complicated in a world that is tilting toward nationalism and ultra-nationalism over globalism and globalization. The world outside looks less secure, threatening, and unpredictable. Trade agreements, like the Trans Pacific Partnership (TPP), are unpopular and no longer a sure thing. In late June 2016, British citizens voted in a slight majority to take an exit (Brexit) from the European Union for a host of reasons that ranged from a loss of British sovereignty to concerns about open borders vis-à-vis refugees and economic migrants. The British pound dropped by ten percent in a matter of hours and Japan's yen became an immediate currency safe haven, playing havoc with Abenomics, Prime Minister Shinzo Abe's answer to Japan's two decades of the economic blahs. On July 1, 2016, ISIS-inspired Bangladeshi terrorists took over the Holey Artisan Bakery in the capital city of Dakha, killing 20 foreign nationals, including seven Japanese contractors with the Japan International Cooperation Agency (JICA). From global trade to global terrorism, soft power–the ability to get what you want through nonviolent and non-aggressive attraction and persuasion—is losing out to aggressive, sometimes violent, means of getting what one wants. Against that backdrop, Japan continues to pivot between steps forward and backward in its international information and communication efforts.

PART I. PROMOTING JAPAN IN THE WORLD

This book is the English-language version of what I hope to see translated into Japanese. My intent is to provide some advice and guidance to my Japanese counterparts in the way that they go about explaining, influencing and engaging with the rest of the world, with a sense of urgency related to the 2020 Summer Olympics, commonly known as Tokyo 2020. In a government context, we call this public diplomacy or diplomacy to publics: how the government informs, engages and influences citizens in foreign countries. In a world of iPhones, social media and social networks (Facebook, Twitter, Instagram, Line) where a token persuasion attempt or reaction comes in the form of a click and emoticon, a nation's promotion—its ongoing reputation and credibility–is increasingly put in the hands of the people, which then becomes person-to-person diplomacy. We end up with a need to examine both traditional and non-traditional approaches to making connections between the citizens of one country with another. I've chosen Japan as my case study. Simply put, Japan's efforts to promote its story in the world have been more of a difficult and annoying struggle than a success. My purpose is to make the efforts more successful, and less burdensome.

Discussing such a broad topic as to how to energize Japan's nation brand image in the world can go one of two ways. One can present a matter-of-fact explanation of how Japan's global communications function and how the powers-that-be might improve it. I do that here, but I offer more. I place Japan's nation brand image and information war campaign in a critical and conflictual context.

I aim to speak diplomatically and encouragingly but also to be true to the many concerns and criticisms that I feel must be aired publicly. These concerns are not just mine. I'm a messenger of what many Japanese people and officials have shared with me privately. Several times I've been told, "We need you," with a knowing look from a Japanese, particularly a woman. I'd hate to think that my efforts here will be misconstrued as "Japan-bashing," a tired phrase from the 1980s that is trotted out for convenience when one wants to shut down any dissension. Further, I'm not here as a Western woman on a rescue mission. Japan's citizens are the primary caretakers of their nation-state. I do realize that my so-called *gaijin* (foreign, non-Japanese) privilege comes with responsibilities to not just partake in that heightened status but also give back.

I'm trained in international relations with a specialization in peace and conflict resolution studies and intercultural and international communication. Over the years I've advanced my doctoral studies with continual research and writing in public diplomacy, global public and media relations, and propaganda studies. I'm very interested in and disturbed by the say-do and perception gaps that pervade the landscape of political culture. Japan is no exception to the rule. Its own gaps are particularly precarious because of Japan's location in one of the world's most militarized areas, combined with its heightened natural disaster propensity and natural resource poverty that feeds the Japanese mindset of *ganbatte*, *ganbaro* (do your best, never give up). In English we might translate that as perseverance, and many Japanese have told me that perseverance in the face of adversity is one of Japan's highest virtues. I would agree. I would add to that positive trait something else that feeds Japan's public diplomacy globally and its domestic politics: passivity and pessimism.

The Japanese people are world-renowned in work ethic, educational preparedness (especially K-12), and devotion to the task at hand. In those respects, they are very active. But in another derivation of active, an "ism" known as activism, the Japanese people are less prepared, absent or ignored. There are exceptions: Japanese far right activists (*uyoku dantai*) thrive and their *gaisensha* sound trucks are a propaganda presence to the eyes of even the most laid-back tourist. But the kind of civic activism that we normally think of as both essential and healthy for a democracy–an engaged citizenry that seeks social and political change for the good of all of its citizens—is missing in impactful numbers.

I am no expert on Japanese high school textbooks, whose sanitized coverage of wartime Japan is becoming a nation brand hazard these days, but I could state with a high degree of confidence that citizen activism is not taught or discussed enough. If students aren't getting the full picture of what their society and its 'warts and all' history is all about, then how can they be expected to act on it or to communicate their collective stories to the world?

The Japanese word for public is *kokyo*, but this definition is used most often in the context of official or governmental public information. A public official (politician) in Japan is viewed as much more important in the everyday workings of the country than a public citizen. Just observe the media narrative and document what stories are carried. Citizens are expected to perform as dutiful, law-abiding citizens in service of society, which isn't wrong, but along with that comes a tendency to not question the system as a whole. What we lose in that non-questioning posture is the ability to solve problems, especially critical social and political problems that require new thinking. Japanese citizen participation in democracy has to improve if Japan's image and reputation in the world is to improve. Japan is so much more than its politicians or its political institutions like its ministries and The Diet; a broader casting of who the Japanese are and what ties them to the rest of the world is a story yet to be told.

In the post-3/11 era of the last five years, Japanese citizens have taken to the streets to protest against nuclear power, changes to the Constitution, or against American military presence in Okinawa. When a Japanese citizen protests against the government, the government tends to respond like it is a political hiccup or headache. Drink a cup of tea, set up security barriers, and the irritant might go away. The tea is the everyday orderliness and public politeness in Japanese society and business-as-usual in government.

When a man set himself on fire end of June 2014 to protest Prime Minister Shinzo Abe's administration proposed constitutional changes,[21] the gruesome spectacle was broadcast widely to social media uplinks on bystander smart phones and in the foreign press. It was not deemed newsworthy enough to receive coverage in the country's most watched public broadcaster, NHK, ostensibly because NHK does not broadcast suicides or attempted suicides. What the "burning man" suicide attempt symbolized at the most desperate level was support for Japan's Peace Constitution, one that has stood firm since 1947 for Japan's most enduring national brand: a pacifist, peace-loving, antiwar nation and state as illustrated in Article 9.[22] His act of civil disobedience also represented a fury of pent-up frustration with Japan's political system that perpetuates with little regard for what the people want. Before setting himself on fire, the man used a megaphone to address the crowd at Shinjuku, one of the world's busiest public transportation stations.[23] It was almost as if he were staging his one-time, one-act spectacle to say, "If I must die, then let me finally have a voice of protest against the direction that my country is going." Jeff Kingston, director of Asian Studies at Temple University Japan, described the self-immolation as the most extraordinary act of political protest he's seen in a quarter of a century of living in Japan.[24]

NHK's blackout of the man's political protest is somewhat understandable if one places *Nippon Hōsō Kyōkai* (Japan Broadcasting Corporation) in the context with which most Japanese generally understand it, as a broadcast organizational arm of the Japanese government. NHK is not such a government mouthpiece. The National Diet, Japan's upper and lower house of elected officials, reviews and approves NHK's considerable annual budget (¥22.5 billion in fiscal 2015). The Diet also appoints NHK's twelve-member Board of Governors. But the funding for NHK comes strictly from reception fees collected from anyone who owns a television. The government is not supposed to have any day-to-day oversight of NHK since it is funded as a public broadcaster (*kokyo hoso*), much like the British Broadcasting Corporation (BBC). As Ellis S. Kraus describes it, "NHK is an independent broadcast agency, and on paper at least, perhaps the freest in the democratic world. Autonomous from, but somewhat accountable to, government may be a good way to characterize the position of NHK."[25] The emphasis is on government-free autonomy.

Today, NHK is more recognized than ever as the broadcast face of Japan nationally and internationally, and yet its reputation as a government broadcaster beholden to government oversight, particularly some of the more divisive policies of the Abe government, is growing. This is why NHK's presence in Japan's communication in the world is central.[26] If Japan wants to be a global player, then it will have to make its independent broadcast agency and its flagship global broadcasting entity, NHK World, a much more visible representation of Japan as a global nation-state. At present, Japan's broadcasting flagship has a long way to go and will continue to struggle with its global orientation, notwithstanding the regional demand for some popular programs like the 2013 hit *Amachan*, which has been rebroadcast with subtitles in Taiwan, Indonesia, Myanmar, Thailand, and most recently, the Philippines.[27]

The pages that follow will challenge Japan to open its doors wider and build its bridges longer. Japan has so much to give to the world; it just doesn't realize it or is too modest to say. As an American, and one especially outspoken (no wilting flower), I have no inhibitions in boasting about Japan, but I'm no good to my host country if all I do is jump on the bandwagon with the readily available Japanophiles and Japan cheerleaders. Being an honest critic is the best way to show friendship. Japan needs to expand its nation brand in the world responsibly and proactively, and not remain such a well-kept secret.

JAPAN'S INFORMATION WAR WITH ITSELF

When visitors first come to Japan, there is an almost textbook description to who the Japanese are and what Japan is. The Japanese people are nice and live in an *omotenashi* culture that puts a premium on taking care of the guest without instruction or overt communication. Japan is safe. Japan is maneuverable, especially if you are like most foreign visitors who stick to the Tokyo-Osaka-Kyoto itinerary. The Japanese people are helpful. Even if there is a communication divide, someone will help you find your way back to your hotel or locate the nearest subway station. Japan is convenient. You can grab a hot or cold coffee just about anywhere, and buy a ready-to-eat spaghetti dinner, *onigiri,* or salad at 7-Eleven or Lawson. You'll never be far from creature comforts, especially in the large urban areas where most of Japan's population resides. We all, foreign visitor and citizen alike, seem to swim along in a frictionless, water-like environment with ritualistic predictability, which is why it is possible for a foreigner to remain here for many years without a firm grasp of the native language.

The penultimate symbol of modern Japan's image, both inside and in the world, is the Japanese bullet rail system, which kept its stellar safety record on Friday, March 11, 2011, with not one person injured or killed, or even one train damaged in the 9.0 magnitude earthquake. A friend from the Ministry of Foreign Affairs who oversees Japan's public diplomacy was especially pleased to share that statistic with me when I was here on a Fulbright a year after 3/11. It is something to be proud of, along with the patient and respectful manner in which the majority of people behaved in the weeks and months that followed the triple disaster.

In Japan, trains don't just run on time, with spoken and visible apologies from train conductors if they are late, but they also unite Japan's modern with traditional, new with old. A *shinkansen* can easily drop you off in Kyoto city center, where you can access 1,600 temples and 17 World Heritage site properties. In Japan, old isn't just about people; it's a point of pride about cultural and national identity.

In contrast, in the United States it's more likely for people to prefer the new over the fairly new. It's not uncommon to buy a new car every few years. When I first moved to Southern California after several snowy winters in New Hampshire, my SoCal native friend said in all seriousness that I would have to buy a newer car because "in California you are what you drive." I just laughed. I still drive my 1998 Honda and am looking forward to its classic car status, if it makes it, which it should. After all, it's a Honda. A car is considered a "classic oldie" after thirty years. In upstate New York I own a 104-year-old American craftsman home and appreciate its history and the past, but how we view the past in the U.S. is quite relative, not absolute.

US-centric tendencies are toward the here and now that carry with them constant adjustment and openness to change. When you consider a country like Japan with its ancestral heritage extending to 35,000 years ago when the first inhabitants occupied the Japanese archipelago, there is a natural orientation to the past and the way you've always done things. Japan is very westernized in a lot of its appearance, and the Japanese people continue to look to the West (US, UK, France) for education and culture, but the cultural divide is most apparent at the deeper, interpersonal level of communication than what one will encounter in a superficial interaction between a tourist and guide. For instance, the millions of Chinese tourists in Japan are primarily encountered in a shopping context, not as potential cultural interpreters or mediators.

In interpersonal communication, the foreign temporary visitor to Japan will comment about how polite and friendly the Japanese people are, how they smile and seem very easygoing in manner. These observations are accurate. But digging beneath the shiny surface to a level where there may be some disagreement or debate, that's hard, even for a foreigner who has lived here for quite some time. This is because the outside smooth surface is valued more in public life to keep things running along, but if one has an objection, it's hard to speak up.

In Japan, one of the highest values is what we know in the English vernacular as saving face. A face-saving strategy is designed to avoid embarrassment, humiliation or a stain on one's reputation. A Japanese person would know this communicative reality as *tatemae*, but in a much larger societal context. It drives one's everyday life, especially in the workplace, public space or any public encounter. Tatemae is described by Karel van Wolferen in *The Enigma of Japanese Power* as "the way things are presented, ostensible motives, formal truth, the façade, pretense, the way things are supposed to be." Tatemae is highly valued and endemic to Japan's challenges in global communication because it upholds Japan's devotion to harmony (*wa*) and the spirit of the Japanese people. (*Yamato*, or "great harmony," is the oldest name for Japan.) The opposite of tatemae is *honne*, the real truth a person knows inside his heart and mind. Honne—your actual feelings and intentions, are not to be publicly shared because this disclosure can lead to embarrassing situations between people, and therefore, disharmony. Being disharmonious is akin to being un-Japanese, a tough indictment.

Westerners, generally speaking, to the consternation of many a Japanese, are raised to value "spelling things out." As a child growing up in the United States I was told that honesty was the best policy and that if I wanted something I had to speak up. An apt phrase was "the squeaky wheel gets the grease." If you don't make your true intentions known, then you'll be overlooked. Making your intentions known can lead to conflict, but we often think it's better to be heard and understood than to keep our feelings inside where they will only fester and lead to some future outburst.

In Japan, not rocking the boat, or the island, is the best policy. If you are a foreigner, you will be given much wider berth for open expression than a native Japanese, but even foreigners need to appreciate the Japanese love for reserve and not spelling things out. Figuring things out implicitly, the proverbial "reading the air," is preferred. As Alex Kerr writes in *Dogs and Demons: Tales from the Dark Side of Japan*, "People will strive to uphold the tatemae in the face of blatant facts to the contrary, believing it is important to keep the honne hidden in order to maintain public harmony."

The dichotomy between honne and tatemae has led to many an academic article or workshop, particularly regarding how Japanese negotiate in business transactions. My graduate school experience coincided with the bubble economy years of Japan, Inc. right before the bust. Much was made then of the Japanese 'mask' in negotiation, the gap between what was being said or not said publicly and what was really going on. John Pilger said in 1987, "Japan is a nation of masks. Learning to live behind a mask is a prerequisite of much of Japanese civilization." This communication challenge to the West continues today and is written about in books like Jonathan Rice's 2004 book, *Behind the Japanese Mask*. Westerners who view business relations as direct, efficient, and to the point, become frustrated with what seem to be exhausting social obligations surrounding the exchange of information in Japan.

The honne/tatemae dichotomy is especially challenging in Japan's current political communication environment. The dominant political figure, Prime Minister Shinzo Abe, has managed to present himself as the new symbol of Japan to the world in the form of his media-friendly Abenomics and Womenomics. But Abe the man is a career politician who left the prime minister's office in 2007 after just one year in his first term, only to find new life in his second term that began December 2012. His political revival may be good for Japan's visibility in the world, but his narrow-thinking, nationalist politics are not signs of an open, democratic, modern society. Abe is a "special advisor" to a group with a most innocuous name: Nippon Kaigi ("Japan Conference"), that wields incredible persuasive lobbying power in Japan's official narrative. It is highly nationalistic and overtly revisionist about Japan's imperial war behavior in World War II. It goes so far as to view wartime Japan as an East Asian liberator, never an occupier. Japan Conference wants Japan to get rid of its outmoded pacifist Constitution, strengthen its armed forces from defense-only, and teach patriotic and traditional family values, along with a return of a revered and worshipped emperor. The group views the U.S. occupation of Japan and the creation of a new constitution with its war renunciation clause as a period that "emasculated" Japan.[28] Nothing short of a new infusion of political steroids is needed to restore pride and order. Estimates are that one third of Japan's parliament known as The Diet and half of Shinzo Abe's Cabinet are also members of Nippon Kaigi.

Countless Japanese I know tell me privately how disdainful they are of such a reactionary and conservative stance for Japan but these same people would not utter this in polite company. They know that I'm an outsider and a Japan observer—at times a critic—so they feel especially comfortable with sharing their honne feelings. At the macro global communications level, Japan continues to favor tatemae. This does not bode well for Japan's post-3/11 and pre-Tokyo 2020 global public relations. A longtime resident of Japan, Debito Arudo, explains my cause for alarm as it relates to corporate and government malfeasance in general, [29] but especially the foot-dragging surrounding the truth of Fukushima-Daichi radiation:

> What is considered the most untrustworthy of professions? Politics, of course. Because politicians are seen as personalities who, for their own survival, appeal to people by saying what they want to hear, regardless of their own true feelings. That is precisely what tatemae does to Japanese society. It makes everyone into a politician, changing the truth to suit their audience, garner support or deflect criticism and responsibility.

Arudo believes that it was tatemae that led to public lying about the post-Fukushima Daiichi Nuclear Power Plant radioactive realities. Such a strong orientation to save face can, at its worst, lead to non-disclosure and cover-up over a full airing of what is really going on behind the scenes.

DECONSTRUCTING COOL JAPAN

Japan has a soft power projection to the world that stems from attraction to its entertainment and popular culture. Collectively known as "Cool Japan" or Kūru Japan, the industries involved include Japanese fashion (e.g. Harajuku, Lolita), J-Pop girl groups like AKB48, as well as manga (comic books), anime (animation), and cosplay (costume play based on animation characters). Targeted primarily at a younger demographic overseas, the commercial popular culture industries are receiving the most focused press attention in the Cool Japan campaign of recent years. It is understood that Japan has both a traditional and modern culture that attracts global interest, but Cool Japan has a 21st century edge to its promotion with a dominant emphasis on global youth culture appeal through Japan origin entertainment.

The Japanese government started to formally adopt a pop culture approach in its diplomacy to global publics when it first used the term "public diplomacy" in its Diplomatic Bluebook 2004. To be sure, Japan's culture power status began decades earlier. Post-World War II Japan could not exercise hard power options, so it relied on soft power agendas (e.g., foreign aid, cultural diplomacy, person-to-person exchanges), primarily to the United States and ASEAN member countries. The Japan Overseas Cooperation Volunteer (JOCV) program began in 1965 and was modeled on the U.S. Peace Corps. Another cornerstone of Japan's cultural diplomacy is the Japan Exchange and Teaching (JET) program. The Japan Foundation was founded in 1972 to coordinate the country's cultural diplomacy and exchange activities.

In the mid-1970s, after anti-Japanese riots took place in Bangkok, Thailand and Jakarta, Indonesia against then Prime Minister Tanaka Kakuei, Japan launched a national image campaign that resulted in the Fukuda Doctrine pledge to reestablish "heart to heart relations" with Southeast Asia. The Japan Foundation, with a budget of over US $150 million, has 24 overseas offices in 23 countries and continues to pursue a strong cultural diplomacy agenda that began with the Fukuda Doctrine. By the mid-2000s, Japan relied on cultural products (Cool Japan) and cultural diplomacy (Japan Foundation) for the bulk of its public diplomacy. Despite a slowing of the domestic economy that began in the 1990s, Japan's popular culture still held a superpower status that was marked by an increase in demand for modern cultural products. A 2002 *Foreign Affairs* article by Douglas McCray ("Japan's Gross National Cool") helped to inspire the culture-first approach while Japan was still reeling from its first decade of economic decline.

Cool Japan as a governmental global promotional campaign kicked off officially on November 25, 2013 when I attended--in a sea of older male government ministry officials--the opening ceremony of the Cool Japan Fund headquarters in the Roppongi Hills Complex, one of Tokyo's swankiest locales. Nobuyuki Ota, the founding CEO of Cool Japan Fund,[30] describes it as a "private collaboration"[31] based on the following belief:

> We believe that one of our roles is to promote the "Made Locally, Sold Worldwide" ideal, and to do so we aim to unearth some of the amazing products being made around the country. By encouraging companies selling those products to expand their businesses overseas, we can contribute to the revitalization of local communities nationwide.
>
> If we can help nurse those communities back to greater economic health, we may see an increase in foreign visitors wishing to see the beautiful towns and villages of Japan. Those visitors will return home and perhaps tell others about their wonderful experiences of Japanese lifestyle, culture, and hospitality, and that will potentially help improve Japan's image as a whole.

A collective called the Cool Japan Movement Promotion Council (hereinafter, "the Council") issued a report in 2014 that began with the following study questions: (1) What does it mean for Japan to win the sympathy of other countries? (2) What more can Japan do now to create such a state? What they concluded was that Japan was slow on the go with its own global promotional campaigns, despite the obvious demand for all things Japan.

An acknowledged tone of defeat encapsulated the report: "Meanwhile, the Cool Japan movement has not proven very effective in achieving its original purpose of winning the sympathy of other countries toward Japan."

The Council report states this presumption: "Every Japanese person must have heard of the phrase, 'for the good of the world and the good of people.' Winning the world's sympathy may be related to the virtue of working for others that the Japanese people have inherently possessed since ancient times." And thus was born this mission principle of Cool Japan: Japan, a Country That Provides Creative Solutions To the World's Challenges.

Rhetorically speaking, the Council report talks about Cool Japan in the context of win-win global solutions and not just one-way nation brand promotion, which is good because one-way communication strategies are always destined to fail.

Most notable was the realization that "the issues that Japan faces ahead of the rest of the world will certainly arise in other countries." These include a rapidly aging society, dying local communities, food supply and environmental concerns related to global capitalism. To that end, Cool Japan may have a noble purpose in offering innovative solutions that help the world and thereby enhance Japan's global image.

Cool Japan's projected aim is to create "a national movement encouraging the Japanese people to fully exercise their voluntary creativity in the international community." But how does it do that and what exactly does it deliver? A few revelations can be found at the Cool Japan website (http://www.cj-fund.co.jp), that also lists Cool Japan investments. These include an overseas Japan Channel, a US-based Japanese Tea Café, and a Japan Food Town project in Singapore, the latter which is expected to "have a number of knock-on effects, increasing people's familiarity with Japan's rich food culture around the world, increasing the number of fans of Japanese cuisine, and increasing the number of visitors to Japan."

The proposed Japan Channel is a joint venture with the already existing overseas channel, "Wakuwaku Japan," responsible for broadcasting AKB48 concerts and documentaries to overseas audiences. This joint venture, according to a Cool Japan Fund press release, "will propose the following attractive experiences toward broadcasted countries' Japan freaks in cooperation with a myriad of Japanese companies; music live events featuring with popular Japanese performers, friendly matches between a J-league club with a local league one, or fashion related events with Japanese fashion goods sale." My conclusion: Expect more AKB48 concerts..

One of the action recommendations in the Council report was to replace Cool Japan with another name or phrase and to listen more to native English speakers, to which I could not agree more:

> Present a phrase that replaces Cool Japan, which tends to be perceived as being not cool for calling ourselves "cool." Listen to the opinions of native English speakers and feedback from both within and outside of Japan, and propose a phrase that concisely expresses the brand value of Japan and can be used proudly by the Japanese people.

A.T. Kearney's Tak Umezawa is a Cool Japan strategist who calls for Cool Japan to embrace 'remixing cultures' and to focus on what overseas people are interested in discovering about Japan:

> Japan has imported foreign cultures on a grand scale throughout its history – in ancient days from the Korean peninsula and China, later on from Europe, and from the USA since the end of the war – and then sublimated them all into Japanese culture. Like a DJ creating a remix of a song, Japan has continued to create new value by remixing cultures. Continuously introducing foreign cultural elements and maintaining the cultural diversity is vital to this dynamic process.

> If we stick to the idea of "Japanese-ness" too much, we may end up with promoting what is deemed to be "correct Japanese content" while ignoring what people overseas are interested in. Just laying out high-quality Japanese goods in front of the overseas consumers is not enough

to succeed in the global market. It requires never-ending innovations of the content and effective curation to communicate its value. [32]

Umezawa shows a deeper understanding of nation branding than I've generally encountered thus far in Japan. Nation branding is a process whereby you can end up treating the nation either as a corporate entity or as a commodity of promotion in the world. In order to save the soul of the nation, the branding, a form of global public relations, requires a carefully thought-out strategy or plan of action. The issue for Japan is that it has not worked out such a strategy. It has defined neither goals nor values.

Branding is to nations as personality is to individual persons – it is just a 'face' and it rationalizes the contradictions of what "We the People," be they Japanese, American, Malaysian, actually are. Where it can no longer do that rationalization, then it fails. Nation branding is never quite true in an absolute sense. Either it must be revised or the contradictions must be dealt with. The latter is the better option, where the values projected are valid and the contradictions are addressed.

An ongoing problem for Japan is that the people who often get placed in global promotion campaigns tend to default on usual suspect initiatives from Japan's "pink soft power"[33] messaging of Hello Kitty and J-Pop (popular culture) to its rather abstruse *omotenashi*. Japanese economics professor Nobuhiro Ikeda explained omotenashi (loosely understood as Japan's service, hospitality style) as not easily transferable to other countries, which is a problem if you are trying to promote your country around the world. What you need are global consumers who come to you based on clear expectations:

The question of whether "omotenashi" is adaptable to other countries is answerable with the original Japanese word "kaizen." The master and pupil relationship and "kaizen" demand that the producer and the consumer engage in a long-term learning relationship, that is, in a relational paradigm. A producer and a consumer must constantly learn from each other to obtain the required experience, knowledge, intelligence, and insight.[34]

As Tokyo-based writer Philip Brasor observes, when the global visitors do come in the vein of "it's unique to Japan," omotenashi can be a bit inflexible, as he explains in his point about a traditional Japanese inn:

> The idea of omotenashi here is that the guest does not have to ask for service and thus doesn't feel as if he or she is imposing on anyone, but many people prefer to set their own eating and sleeping itineraries when they travel. Staying in a ryokan can be a rich and, yes, unique experience, but for most foreign travelers — as well as quite a few Japanese I know — once is enough.[35]

All this talk about omotenashi pre-Tokyo 2020 makes one nostalgic for a Japan that was able to penetrate the collective consciousness of the world when it had no competition from China, South Korea, Taiwan, or any number of other Northeast Asian neighbors. At one time, Japan's message was bold and proud. Think Akio Morita when he was President of Sony, whose message to the world was: "We're creative, smart, and we make stuff to make your life better." And thus was born, "It's a Sony." Morita appeared in a 1985 American Express commercial[36] six years after the release of the first Walkman and his face inside a Sony TV graced the cover of *Time* weekly magazine on May 10, 1971 with the ominous headline, "How to Cope with Japan's Business Invasion." The article describes a man destined to change the nation brand image of his country:

> In 1953, a young businessman named Akio Morita made his first trip outside Japan to investigate export prospects for his struggling little electronics company. He was dismayed to find that in the sophisticated markets of the U.S. and Europe, the words Made in Japan were a mocking phrase for shoddiness. But in The Netherlands, he recalls, "I saw an agricultural country with many windmills and many bicycles,

and yet it was producing goods of excellent quality and had worldwide sales power. I thought that maybe we Japanese could do it too.[37]

Morita was one of Japan's first brand champions but his legacy is mostly forgotten today since Sony's share of the global electronics market is not as a leader but an also-ran in the shadow of China and Korea. Morita should not be forgotten. He spoke English well, traveled widely, and wherever he went upheld the Japanese social contract, consensus-building and reliability, so that people everywhere concluded that the Japanese were peaceful, hardworking and cooperative. The bumper sticker impression: Japanese: Nice people. Get stuff done. Make good stuff.

Then there is Konosuke Matsushita, the founder of Panasonic, who pushed the social responsibility ethic of Japanese companies to make things that people need. Japan's culture at this time was seen as at a level of magic and awe, not kitschy *kawaii* soulless, mouthless, like Hello Kitty. Japan at the time of this industry leader produced stuff that people around the world really wanted but also cultivated an attraction for traditional Japanese culture that elevated the human spirit–the martial arts, pottery making, Zen, and kimono.

The problem with omotenashi today is that too many marketing and advertising people have tried to translate it to the world– to make it understandable in the mundane terms of some kind of elevated hotel hospitality – which cuts away all the Japan magic that came with the era of the company men like Matsushita and Mori. They understood Japan's connection to the world and could translate it on their own terms.

Japan has lost its magical edge and it won't get it back if it keeps promoting the juvenile proto-sexuality of J-Pop singers like AKB48 who may have a replicable footprint outside of Japan, but who also manage to dilute Japan's sophisticated edge. Cosplay is everywhere now, but so is violent manga and anime. It is not all *Rilakkuma* ("bear in relaxed mood.")

NATION BRAND JAPAN

BEYOND COOL

When exactly did Japan become "cool" anyway? It was cool long before the *New York Times* or Douglas McGray came up with the idea ("Japan's Gross National Cool") – back in pre-Bubble days when everybody was talking about the "Japan Miracle" – back when Sony's Akio Morita was on the cover of *Time* and American businesses were trying to emulate Japanese organizational principles. That's when sushi caught on – along with Japanese martial arts – and manga and anime. Japan had rebuilt itself, its technology was second to none, and it had established itself as the model of a peaceful, non-violent state that just wanted to make life better. As with Cool Britannia, Japan's popularity worldwide grew from the culture itself, without the help of marketing, and it was based on real accomplishments.

Is Japanese food popular? Yes, some kinds of Japanese food, most obviously sushi or Benihana Teppanyaki-style grilling are globally popular, but so are Thai, Mexican, Indian, Spanish and Chinese. The popularity of Japanese food has more to do with the overall popularity of ethnic foods than Japanese culture itself. Vancouver, Canada has a lot of sushi restaurants, many run by Koreans and Chinese.

Every nation brand feature is a story waiting to be told. For Japan, it's no different. Japan's nation brand story has yet to be told. It is not being told through Cool Japan and it is not being told through its people. To market anyone, you have to tell a personal story, with a beginning, middle and end, characters, their motivations, values, moral, and passion. It needs to be true but it also needs to appeal to its audience with compelling, powerful, irresistible detail.

Cool Japan doesn't work particularly well because there is no story that holds one's attention. There are popular and commercial stories for mass consumption purposes, but not necessarily personal stories.

Cool Britannia worked because it was a story before it got the attention of advertising people and the Blairites. Cool Japan leads with government bureaucrats and advertising. The Japanese ad people copped what they thought was a 'cool' slogan – and then looked for content. "How are we cool? Oh, Americans like sushi and anime and manga. I guess it's that." But where's the story? Who are the heroes? Who are the villains? How did it start? What are the challenges?

Cool Britannia had a real story – with real heroes – the Beatles, Sex Pistols, Richard Branson, all fighting the Establishment, discovering freedom and equality in a not-very-free and not-very-equal society, creating something new. Youth culture was emphasized, both evolutionary, revolutionary. The beginning was the 60s. The end was Tony Blair.

Of course Japan has a story too. It's just that no one has told it.

Cool Britannia involved a countercultural narrative (like all art), egalitarian and actually subversive of established order, which meant it was difficult to government institutionalize. It was a bit like a good video game, but bigger and more complex. Cool Japan has no countercultural narrative – even though such memes are sprinkled throughout anime, manga, and Japanese art generally. Cool Japan downplays the story or stories underlying the emergence of anime or manga or even the pedophilian-themed girl bands. Japanese popular art is dominated by certain themes – violence, sexuality, regression, escape – as you might expect in a conformist, quasi-authoritarian society. But Cool Japan pretends that those themes do not exist – it's all "cool" as in "Just chill, man."

It is ironic that in a country like Japan that is famous for its consensus-driven society, there is no modern "national story," unlike the early 1970s when the narrative was Japan as the Phoenix, as in *Hi no Tori*. At least that was something and projected a rising Japan with infinite power. As Anime Network describes *Hi no Tori*: "every story teaches a lesson: Life is beginning of an eternity, a never-ending cycle."

In effect, the Abe administration and the Ministry of Economy, Trade and Industry (METI), which oversees Cool Japan, are trying to co-opt an underlying cultural frustration, which increases apace with Japanese economic and social inequality, renaming it "Cool Japan." But this time it is more about Japanese Golden Triangle elites trying to gain membership into the club of global elites. The tribe these Cool Japan managers belong to is not in any way like the tribes that ordinary people belong to.

Japan has so many positive things going for it and it has had some impressive personalities in positions of power. Certainly Matsushita was one. One problem for the Abe administration is that it takes its instructions on 'soft power' influence from too many people who are very insufficiently trained in marketing, social science, communications, public relations, public diplomacy or even advertising. And they tend to wear cultural blinders. It also tends to listen to sycophants more than dissidents and you need both for any party (or global communication program) to be interesting.

The best people to advise the Japanese about soft power are globalists who recognize the values, products and services that Japanese take for granted. Globalists tend to ignore the culturally doctrinal refuse and keep the good stuff. Listen to the global nomads more. There's an old Kim Carnes' song called "Bette Davis Eyes." Let's change that to "Foreign Eyes" in relation to Japan's soft power embrace with the world. The best people to advise the Japanese are often, but not exclusively, foreigners. We see things that native Japanese may take for granted and we weed out what is culturally of little importance to the rest of the world. It's why I would stack the group with foreigners if I were running a Cool USA counterpart.

The foreign eyes/ears don't necessarily have to be Japan specialists, which is why I tend to believe that Japan House, a new public diplomacy initiative of the Ministry of Foreign Affairs, holds much more promise than typical government-standard issue soft power initiatives. It relies on a local secretariat, specialists and community leaders from the private and nonprofit sector, to decide the programming, people whose expertise is in the communities (Los Angeles, Sao Paolo, London) where the Japan House will reside.[38]

If the Japanese government wanted Japanese popular culture to be more successful abroad, it would have to create the conditions for popular culture to rise above its present level of risible mediocrity. It's a given that the Japanese produce high quality products. But why is it that Japan hasn't produced many really memorable movies since the 50s and 60s? Australia, with one-fifth the population, does so much better. Why do Japanese TV dramas deflate the senses? New Zealand, with just 5 million people, seemingly does better than Japan for film and TV location and storytelling. Why isn't Japan's pop music in the Top 100 globally? Finland, also with just 5 million, does as well or better with its world and folk music.

I'm not a film aficionado but I'm a fan of the films of Yasujiro Ozu and Akira Kurosawa, whose work influenced some of the world's best directors like John Ford and Wim Wenders.

When I was teaching as a Fulbright professor at Sophia University in 2012, I had the chance to watch Ozu's classic *Tokyo Story* for the first time. I asked my Japanese students if they loved the film as much as I did—with its universal themes of family strife and generational divides–and they looked at me with blank faces. Likewise, they had no knowledge of Kurosawa's background as a painter, which led him to storyboard his film scenes as paintings. I realize that Japanese textbooks tend to sanitize Japan's wartime history, but what better way to reenergize the youth and their place in the world than classes in Japan's Golden Age of Cinema.

There is plenty of talent here in Japan, and loads of creativity, but it has no place to go. The people calling the shots are largely educated at a couple of universities, mostly Todai, Waseda and Keio, with degrees in economics and political science, which amount to four years, reading a few books, and spending ample time drinking or in social clubs. Okay, I exaggerate to make a point, but I'm not altogether impressed with what is being taught across the curriculum or impressed by the level of intellectual commitment to learning the great works. Yoshio Sugimoto describes the Japanese university as a "moratorium," explaining further:

> While primary and secondary education in Japan produces highly trained pupils, Japan's universities remain a resting space or 'leisure land' for many youngsters. Exhausted, both mentally and physically, by

examination hell, they seek relaxation, enjoyment, and diversion in their university life. University students spend an average of only thirty-four minutes per day studying outside the classroom, while middle and high school pupils in their final years spend approximately one hour and ten minutes on average. Japanese students can afford to be lazy because Japanese firms hire university graduates, not so much on the basis of what and how much they have studied, as on the hensachi ranking of their university.[39]

On top of this, the Ministry of Education proposed an evisceration of the humanities and the social sciences in summer 2015 just at a time when Japan needs to expand its brainpower in problem solving, debate, philosophy, and critical thinking. The Ministry of Education wants to put more focus on "practical" and "vocational" needs of Japan to help boost the economy, as if all Japan needs is an economic injection of humanoids whose task are to create a better nation-state for consumerism and capitalism. After much outcry, the Ministry pulled back on its original declaration, but the damage had been done in the suggestion. The unexamined life, well, we know, what that leads to.

To be fair, the United States of America isn't much better with its cultural programming, with the movie and TV industry dominated by a few companies, but there is still greater competition than Japan, thanks to a plethora of channels, including cable, which demands content and therefore receives imports from other countries. There is also Sundance and a vibrant documentary and independent film movement. Not so Japan. Japan's popular culture is concentrated and it seems to cater to lower brow mass-market tastes, including a lot of cooking shows and infomercials. More than half of Japan's population lives in just two metropolitan areas, the Kanto and the Kansai region, and the creative impulses play to these markets.

Assuming that conditions for the development of media independent of the corporatocracy are not going to change, Japan should be focusing on introducing its culture in terms of primary values, namely, the importance of social harmony and a social contract built on consensus and cooperation. These are the basic values of the village, in which no one is left behind and all are provided for. As social inequality increases, these values are gradually being undermined, but they are still in force.

So far, Japan is promoting the culture too much and too often as a commodity. It is hard to "promote" a culture – it must essentially sell itself without seeming like a sale. So you must provide access to it. This is a little hard for the ever-insular Japanese. Japanese manufacturers tend to leave promotion and marketing to local subsidiaries. Head office marketing focuses instead on corporate values like reliability, organization, efficiency, and technology development. A company's global identity culture is best when very generally defined in terms of values that are universal or almost universal.

The United States has its universal icons like the Statue of Liberty or Mount Rushmore. Otherwise: Life, Liberty and the Pursuit of Happiness might as well be the slogan for the National Brand of the USA that are able to transcend and inspire the world over, even if U.S. behavior and actions in the world don't match those ideals. Ideals, like ideas, still matter. Sony's classic ad copy, "It's a Sony," was a superb slogan for all of Japan. It implied pride, uniqueness, creativity, and high status all at the same time, without any didactic message. That was Sony's culture, and it connected with the world. Who didn't feel a little kinship with the Japanese when buying a Walkman? I know that I wanted to thank Japan for giving this music lover portable enjoyment.

Japan today, without Morita, is about *wa* ("harmony"). It is a village society, emphasizing peaceful interaction, consensus and the like. But the Japanese are also fun, and that fun should be a big part of their accessibility. Achieving this kind of Japanese harmony requires a high degree of tolerance for escapist activities and fantasy life. So yeah, you can drink and act like a child as a middle-age adult because it's all tolerated in Japan. Underneath all this "wa" is a lot, and I mean tons, of escape from reality. Look at all the Love Hotels ("No Tell" hotels) dotting the landscape. Manga and anime fantasize the supernatural and primal, which is why they are popular as niche media outside Japan.

Japan needs to think of "rebranding" itself in 21st Century terms. To do that, it needs to rely on foreigners who have a more objective view and often a better understanding of Japanese culture, at least from the needs and wants of the consumer who is going to buy what the Japanese are selling. Successful Japanese companies, and successful Korean and European companies, do their marketing using non-native informants. Japan needs to use more non-native informants who have Japan's interests at heart and who are here for the long run. These are not necessarily the foreigners who have gone native, but those foreigners who can serve as an effective bridge between Japan and the world. And Japan needs bridge building for some contested issues.

Japan manages cultural presentation very well in some areas like cuisine and design. It has not managed the international whaling fiasco well. It has not managed the Comfort Woman issue well, much less the Senkaku/Diaoyu Islands. Domestically speaking, the passage of the new security bills that override Article 9 have been disastrous for Prime Minister's Abe popularity (but not his party), and also a taint on the Japan peace brand. The List goes on. Japanese leaders are increasingly seen less positively than before. Soft Power Japan—when politics and history are involved–has lost a lot since the 70s when Japan's nation brand transcended its wartime and post-war identity and became an economic kingpin.

To complicate the soft power projection of Japan, young people in Japan are lagging behind their counterparts in terms of confidence, which seems to correlate with individual creativity and self-initiative. Japan's young people doubt themselves and their future, at least according to one survey conducted by Japan's Cabinet Office in 2013. The survey measured young people's self-esteem and future expectations in seven countries: Japan, South Korea, United States, Britain, Germany, France and Sweden. The Japanese youth between the ages of 13 and 29 ranked at the bottom, including if they thought they would be happy at age 40. They came in last for recognizing their good points. Just 45.8 percent of the Japanese respondents felt confident, while over 70 percent of their counterparts said the same.[40] A majority of Japanese youth (61.6 percent) expressed bright hopes for the future, but other countries' youth exceeded 80 percent. This suggests a hope gap that needs addressing in Japan's schools, including a need for more global literacy, English as a global second language, as well as study of other country's languages and cultures. Open up the world to Japan's youth and you might see a confidence leap.

Imagine what Japan's youth and marketing types would learn if they just realized that hospitality and gracious manners are not exclusive to Japan. I can recall working with an Arab exchange student from Saudi Arabia. I tutored her in university subjects at American University while I was in graduate school at the School of International Service working on my doctorate. If I complimented her on something, she more than likely gave it to me. Once she went to Paris for vacation and returned with a shopping bag of gorgeous haute couture fashion pieces as a "thank you" for my services beyond the $20/hour I was already receiving. In other words, Arab cultures have a long tradition in which their own version of 'hospitality" and honoring the guest is a central value. It is clearly enshrined in the Qu'ran.

Japan should study the omotenashi values of other countries and then present them with Japan's ideas about hospitality, which differ in some respects, but not others. As a marketing and advertising consultant in Tokyo told me, he advises the Japanese to approach their marketing campaigns in a win-win approach. They should adopt the following outlook: "Look, we share these traditions. Our version is most relevant to institutions, rather than personal relationships, and it emphasizes preparations and planning. Yours is personal and open-ended, spiritual and moral, emphasizing personal warmth and integrity. Combining the two traditions we get something special." My friend's advice like this was rejected in a case that focused on having the Japanese "train" their Arab business partners in omotenashi, as though the Arabs knew nothing about service and hospitality. The Arabs took offense at this lack of cross-cultural understanding.

Ironically, Japanese culture is itself mostly derivative. This is not often acknowledged, but it should be since it points to Japan's prowess in acting as a hybrid culture par excellence. Tea and tea ceremony? China and Korea. Japanese kanji? China. Government? The US. Clothing? Often Western-inspired. Music? Again, Western-dominated. Of course, the Japanese adapt culture, as everyone else does. Culture is dynamic, interactive, and continually evolving. Yeah, the world loves Hello Kitty. In summer 2014, Syrian rebel leader of Jaish Al-Islam, Zahran Alloush, whose troops were battling ISIS forces, was pictured speaking to his forces with a Hello Kitty notebook at the lectern. The image went viral, but that didn't stop the murdering of innocent Japanese by ISIS in January 2015. Policy is policy, no matter how despicable and vile it may be, and no pop culture intrusion is going to save someone's life. It's still the policy, stupid.

We are often drawn to a place first in my minds, then in our hearts, and then in our wallets. Promoting culture often fails. What's on all the little maps I see when I'm going to meet someone. Access. It's the map equivalent of Point of Sale in marketing terms. Japan needs to provide more access, more windows into its culture, more points of sale, but in doing so it needs to tell more stories that build emotional connections. Japan does things differently, which gives it its charm, but it needs to allow global publics to first see the culture on their own terms, not lectured at or directed in what to see. And after Japan has been briefed and critiqued by people who came from elsewhere to reside in Japan–your greatest promoters—well next comes Japan's most powerful persuaders and public diplomats–the Japanese people.

NO SEX: BRAND JAPAN STEREOTYPES

Japan suffers from a condition perhaps more than any other country: overcoming negative stereotypes in the media. It's a two-pronged struggle: (1) Japan's weakness in media relations and nation branding management puts the ball in the competitors' court (Korea, China) or in the global public opinion court (foreign press); and (2) Japanese weakness in global English, the language of the foreign press and global public relations, leaves a vacuum for communicators and writers to fill, including fly-by-night editors and journalists who cannot wait to parachute in to Shibuya Crossing and announce, "Japan is so different from any other country in the world."[41]

This Japan Exceptionalism (aka *Nihonjinron*) myth perpetuates, but it is not the style of American Exceptionalism, which is more political. Japan's "otherness" is more cultural and historical, nourished largely by the Japanese themselves, who perpetuate exceptionality to the rest of Asia, and who are dichotomously in awe of the West, particularly the United States, but do not want to be seen as part of the West or the world. Author Peter N. Dale, a rare critic of the Nihonjinron literature, (*The Myth of Japanese Uniqueness*) places Nihonjinron exceptionalism in the context of political conformity and nationalism. It is a mythos for political advantage:

First, they implicitly assume that the Japanese constitute a culturally and socially homogeneous racial entity, whose essence is virtually unchanged from prehistoric times down to the present day. Secondly, they presuppose that the Japanese differ radically from all other known peoples. Thirdly, they are conspicuously nationalistic, displaying a conceptual and procedural hostility to any mode of analysis which might be seen to derive from external, non-Japanese sources. In a general sense then, nihonjinron may be defined as works of cultural nationalism concerned with ostensible 'uniqueness' of Japan in any aspect, and which are hostile to both individual experience and the notion of internal socio-historical diversity.[42]

My lasting impression when I visited Japan in 1993 and 1994 was that Japan seemed like the Germany of Asia in cleanliness, cultural superiority, orderliness, and similar aggressive military past. I also viewed Japan in the context of a "chosen" people, modest, polite but very proud of their distinctiveness and separation from the rest of Asia, this despite a language and culture that is Asia-derivative. However incomplete those first impressions were, they must have been influenced by how the Japanese presented themselves to me, because I had never formally studied Japanese history, culture, or politics.

Because of this common currency toward uniqueness, it's rare that you will hear any discussion in Japan about an East Asian or Northeast Asian identity. The Japanese do not identify positively or orient themselves in the least with the Koreans or the Chinese, despite having much in common. As Jean-Pierre Lehman writes in *The Globalist*:

On the surface, the Northeast Asian trio should have everything going for close union. China, Japan and Korea are each other's major trade and investment partners and their economies are highly interdependent.

Furthermore, they share a common culture. All three are Confucianist societies for which the most prized value is "harmony." Chinese, Japanese and Koreans not only have significant common interests, they should also be able to understand each other on the basis of a common cultural wavelength.[43]

As Lehman and many other scholars point out, it's Japan's history—its break from the East and tilt toward the West that has left it in Asia but not of Asia. With the likely changes to the US-Japan Security Alliance, the break from Asia will become complete and Japan will have chosen the West over the East, specifically the United

States, as its main ally. This causes me some alarm because I believe that Japan's best opportunity to globalize and become a genuine global partner will require some independence from the U.S. in order to reestablish its credibility in the East Asian region.

In Japan, when we aren't taking pictures of our food or talking about how long the lines are for Kukuruza Popcorn or Garrett Popcorn in Omotesando, we have many discussions about what it means to be Japanese versus something else: Korean, Chinese, Westerner, European, Australian, etc. In other words, you are Japanese or you are not. Japan is not an assimilation culture. Japan is a separation culture.

This socialization process toward a mythos of homogeneity fans the flames of distorted media reports that play up Japan's otherness, usually what makes it an oddball outlier.

Our beloved Japan, then how do we market you to the world? We know it as a super nice and safe place where robots, small pets, and cuddle cafes have replaced the government's obsession for more babies in the national interest. Alarming news coverage pervades and propagates, causing alarm and freakish media stories of panic. In 2010, the Ministry of Health, Labour and Welfare released a survey that indicated 36% of Japanese young men between the ages of 16 and 19 had no interest in sex whatsoever. The country is as famous for shrinkage at all levels as it is for natural disasters.

The *Economist* magazine calls Japan a "demographic time bomb" and "the incredible shrinking country."[44] The British Broadcasting Corporation, the most trusted international broadcaster in the world, declares Japan to be a nation of sexless homogeneity in a 2013 special report with a not so nice title, "No Sex Please, We're Japanese." The real *Tokyo Drift* isn't part of the *Fast and Furious* series. It's a slow separation between men and women in the real world for sex and social partners in the virtual world.[45]

In defense of the BBC, the title may have come from a widely panned yet popular 1970s play and film called "No Sex Please, We're British."[46] Nevertheless, when you live for some time in Japan, you cannot avoid these global media impressions that Japan is, as BBC notes from the start, "so different to any other country in the world."

Name any other country that would hold that title. Stereotypes do harm, but they persist, and Japan's stereotypes tussle between the traditional Buddhist temple and Zen garden and schoolgirl fantasies in the men's magazines of the local convenience store. When "No Sex Please, We're Japanese," was released, it launched a media feeding frenzy of print media coverage that bordered on the comical with ping-pong style point-counterpoint pieces:

"Why have young people in Japan stopped having sex?" (*The Guardian*)[47]

"Japan's Hottest New Sex Trend Is Not Having Sex" (*Time*)[48]

"Young People in Japan Have Given Up on Sex" (*Slate*)[49]

"No, Japanese People Haven't Given Up on Sex" (*Slate*)[50]

"Japan's sexual apathy is endangering the global economy" (*Washington Post*)[51]

"Don't worry. The Japanese are having plenty of sex" (*Washington Post*)[52]

In the 2013 special, the BBC's Anita Rani explores the Otaku culture of middle-age nerds and geeks with avatar girlfriends. She peppers the documentary with a few cultural observers like Roland Kelts, author of *Japanamerica*, who takes her on a walk through Akihabara, home to AKB48, the middle-age male fantasy of a dream girl. She walks into a store to pick up adult diapers and claims that Japan now sells more of them than "baby nappies." Rani refers to a random survey that claims only just over a quarter of married Japanese couples have sex once a week. "In one survey," she says, "just twenty percent of them reported having sex every week, way less than us Brits." We in the West might exaggerate such figures of sexual activity while a Japanese modesty value might reduce it, so how reliable are these numbers other than to entertain the viewer and reinforce the image of the Japanese as rather peculiar asexual beings?

So what else do we learn about Japan from the BBC documentary? Japan is full of contradiction. It is one of the most youth-obsessed countries in the world; its media and advertising images are full of doe-eyed youth, mostly female or fembots. In reality, Japan has the highest percentage of old people in the world, who are also female, but not featured in advertising that is targeted especially toward younger female consumers and men of all ages. A quarter of Japanese people are over 65 and are dubbed the "Grand Generation" that created Japan's boom years. To these people who have a lot of pensioner yen to spend, 60 is the new 40. People in their 60s and 70s feel young at heart and BBC's Rani spends time with a group of senior citizen cheerleaders. A 2010 US Census survey showed that there were 53,364 American centenarians, but that was in a nation of 309 million compared to Japan's 127 million, to go along with Greying Japan[53] as opposed to *Fifty Shades of Grey*. Japan is now home to over 60,000 centenarians. The number of Japanese centenarians in 1963, when surveys began, was just 153.

To its credit, the BBC documentary focused as well on Japan's struggle with its lost towns, including Yubari, Japan, once the capital of coal that controlled 90% of the market. After the coal industry died, Yubari turned to a theme park to drum up tourist interest, to a futile end. Yubari holds worldwide fascination as sort of a test case for the future. Current government figures project up to 40% of Japan's cities risk extinction by 2040, which "makes Yubari fascinating as the demographic canary in the Japanese, erm, coal mine."[54]

Population-wise and of most global media interest with 35+ million is Greater Tokyo, which produces a quarter of a million births per year, but not enough for Japan, whose overall birth rate is a stingy 1.3 per woman. In order to replenish Japan's population, the women would need to have at least two babies. Fewer babies translates into fewer future workers, and fewer future workers means fewer taxpayers to pay down the debt. The vicious cycle continues. Japan has seen enormous growth in its unmarried population and just two percent of its babies are born out of wedlock, compared to Great Britain where out-of-wedlock birth is nearly half. But if couples postpone marriage or single people never marry, the babies don't come.

Japan's legendary hospitality aside, its hospitable attitude, according to the documentary, does not extend to foreign residents when compared to other countries. In Great Britain, 1 in 8 residents is born overseas. In Japan, just 1 in 60 residents is foreign-born, roughly 2 percent of the population, but even this low figure refers mostly to the longtime Chinese and Korean generations. That leaves 98 percent ethnically Japanese.

A bizarre twist in the "No Sex Please" documentary, the expected "weird Japan" segment, is a discussion that Rani has with two young men active in an online game called Love Plus, made for Nintendo. It seems very real to its users. It's like going back to dating in high school, but in the documentary one Japanese guy is actually 39 but only 17 in Love Plus. The other guy, who is married, is 38, but a youthful 15 in the game. He keeps his virtual life girlfriend a secret from his wife. "With real life girlfriends you have to consider marriage so I think twice about going out with a 3D (three dimensional) woman." Though he wants to meet a real woman, he's emotionally involved with his virtual GF, Nene.

One scene depicts Rani speaking with a Japanese husband about a virtual girlfriend named Rinko. "If you had to choose between your wife and Rinko, who would you pick?" He hesitates to answer and she laughs with gleeful surprise, reinforcing the image that the Japanese really aren't like you and me. Rinko is part of a trio of virtual girlfriends that Nintendo rolled out in 2009. The game's popularity soared after a young Japanese male married Nene, admitting that he was hooked on her.[55] The wedding was of course not official nor legally binding, but one wonders if marriage rates in Japan would rise if people could marry their virtual partners. It's not too long of a stretch to believe, if we accept the BBC presenter's premise that Japan isn't just different–which it is as much as any foreign country–but also out of this world inhuman, which is implied. One American user of Love Plus described the online 'girls' this way:

Each of these girls is a classic Japanese stereotype. Takane embodies everything about cuteness that Japan finds so attractive, while Nene represents the slightly older and wise classmate, something that Americans can relate to as being sexy as well. Rinko is possibly the most difficult of the three types for a non-Japanese to understand, as she represents the "tsundere" personality type, a girl who is unfriendly and sometimes hostile to people she doesn't know well, but will thaw over time and eventually show her warmer side.[56]

To an outsider, Japanese culture can often be mystifying and confounding. The Japanese schoolgirl uniform, a common outfit in the online and comic book world, is one part titillation and arousal with another part comfort and kawaii. As cultural observer Kelts explains to Rani while walking the main street of Akihabara, "A lot of Japanese adult men remember childhood, particularly school days, as a time of relative freedom, not under the yoke of the boss, not in a tight hierarchy, not taking a train for an hour and a half to your job, and this schoolgirl look is comforting." He adds, "The manga cartoons extend to soft porn levels which can make for uncomfortable public viewing." Does this lack of freedom as an adult help to explain why a 58-year-old Japanese man was arrested in 2016 for "property damage," depositing his semen into the school bags of unsuspecting Tokyo-area high school girls? The charges, which go back several years, came with his explanation that he was "stressed from work."[57]

The sex industry, designed mostly by and for men, thrives in Japan but one Japanese woman, a part-time artist named Megumi Igarashi, was punished by the state for commercially promoting a digital 3D version of her sexual organ. State secrets laws, constitutional ram-throughs, and revisionist history? Okay! A Japanese woman's commercial exploitation of her own body part. Not okay! Confusing, huh? However repugnant Igarashi's stunt is to me personally, I don't think she represented any threat to state or national security that required being arrested.

Where does Japan go from here? Ultimately it seems in the BBC portrait of Japan that men and women just don't fit well together in

Japan's up and down economy years of the last two decades. Boom economy babies were coddled by their mothers, later by their university, and finally by their lifelong employers. Once you were in the system, you were in for life. Today's single Japanese woman may see her male counterpart as deficient. The women of 21st century Japan are becoming more individual and autonomous than their male counterparts. They want something more, their expectations are for something more, and if the men don't deliver, then they won't stay interested. They want men to be independent and more aggressive about dating. Japanese men, in turn, don't like the aggressive women. To add to women's growing power in Japan, they now live to an average age of 88 years, the highest life expectancy in the world, in part due to women's incredible literacy and education, which is number one (highest rank) in the Global Gender Gap Index.[58] Conversely, the Global Gender Gap Report 2015 ranks Japan 101 out of 145 countries, down from 94th place in 2010.[59]

Is there a link between Japan's Otaku (geek, nerd) culture and a declining birthrate? The two men featured in the BBC film think so. There's no opportunity to meet women. No chance, according to the unmarried 39-year-old. People in Japan seem to stay fixated on the youth culture, described as the time when you can be most emotional and free with your feelings without all the responsibility that the work culture brings. Here there is manga culture for anyone at any age. You don't have to grow up. No surprise that Tokyo Disneyland is becoming the most successful Disney theme park (and most visited) in the world.

Is it possible to separate the contradictions in culture that emerge between media hype and everyday life? Yes, if the reporting is responsible, but the BBC special had a tone of "look at these funny people and their funny ways" air about it. Part of the problem lies in a public passivity and apathy as to how the country is played in the foreign media. Unless you are part of the media or someone who covers the media, you may not pay close attention to how the media portray you. Japan needs to do a much better job of talking back to its media, both domestically and internationally.

Against that backdrop, how would you explain Japan in a word, policy, or bumper sticker? Impossible, you say. Well many nations across the globe are investing hundreds of millions into nation brand campaigns to cut through the global communications chatter. So if you were given some of that half a trillion yen to invest in a Beyond Cool Japan campaign, what would you do with it?

To many foreigners whose image of Japan has been reinforced in the media, Japan is out of this world. A friend who visited Japan one time and exclaimed, "Don't you just love Japan? It's the happiest place on earth," might be surprised to be told about Japan's high suicide rate and low rank in global happiness. But on the surface, she's right. Japanese people are polite and smiling and for the casual visitor it wouldn't be a stretch to assume that Tokyo Disneyland is a state of mind here just as much as Japan's belief in its own uniqueness is detrimental to managing its media narrative. For Japan to fully engage the world, it needs to reveal its contradictions. Otherwise there will be only the popularized sunny side up version of Japan and no dark tales to share. How boring is that?

POWER TO THE PEOPLE AND THE PRESS

Japan does not have insurmountable promotion problems different from the rest of the world. It does obsess over its national image at a comparably high intensity, however, which has a lot to do with its world war history, postwar economic middle, and unstable political economy present. Japan was once a top military and imperial regime in control of major parts of Asia as propagated by the Greater East Asia Co-Prosperity Sphere.[60] In the 70s and 80s Japan was the second and vying for first economic power in the world. It believed in its relative superiority long before China surpassed Japan's economic rank in 2010[61] and the U.S. hit an educational exchange milestone in 2014 with more than 100,000 American students in China.[62] That person-to-person milestone between the U.S. and China is sure to have put Japan on final notice that it better act now and not tomorrow to raise its profile in the world.

Given my belief that Japan is a super nation brand with enormous public appeal throughout the world, why hasn't it been able to expand its global footprint in the twenty-first century? It isn't a matter of architecture (visualize government ministry buildings, Dentsu headquarters) and personnel. Big buildings, big staff, but sometimes the most important element—the citizenry—is missing from the conversation.

Japan has not yet reached a critical mass of engagement with the world. It is not enough for Shinzo Abe and Abenomics to grab world press attention. Government heads of state always carry huge sway in how a nation is perceived, but their policy and electoral priorities prevent them from devoting time to a mass scale global persuasion undertaking. These political leaders either enhance or disturb the everyday goings on of a nation and relying on them for a nation's reputation and image is a riskier venture than engaging a critical mass of influential persons in society.[63]

A decentralized and mass scale undertaking is what Japan needs now, not a government central global public relations program given to piecemeal approaches like correcting American textbooks that discuss taboo wartime topics like "comfort women."[64] So far Brand Abe has been too closely aligned with Brand Japan and this is always a precarious alliance when a nation is trying to distinguish itself from its politics. Whatever we want to think of Prime Minister Abe personally (and I have no personal animus toward him), he is a politician promoting some politically divisive policies (constitution reform, media oversight, textbook revising) in areas that impact Japan's global reputation and image, despite his relatively stable popularity numbers at home.

The Japanese people need to be better educated about their citizen ambassador possibilities and encouraged to act on their civic engagement at an international and intercultural level. This doesn't require leaving the country because more foreign visitors are arriving due to the weaker yen that is making a visit to Japan more affordable. Promotion of a country begins at the interpersonal level, but it can be shepherded along from the top.

The Government of Japan realized very late in the game that it had a critical need to internationalize the Japanese campus. In the Greater Tokyo Area university campus, it is common to see the words "global" and "international" used frequently to promote a speaker or course offering. English-language or bilingual signage is becoming more common. Overall, more global curriculum and English-language degree programs are being offered in what was originally named a "Global 30" initiative to double the foreign student population from 140,000 in 2008 to 300,000 by 2020, a total that will be difficult to reach without counting short-term exchanges funded through public-private partnerships such as the TOMODACHI Initiative.[65] The top thirteen Japanese universities that received Global 30 funding had a total of about 22,000 foreign students in 2011, the year of the triple disaster known as 3/11, the same year that the foreign student population dropped to 137,000.[66] As of 2015, that number had increased to 208,379, of which 109,390 originated from two countries in Japan's immediate vicinity: China (94,111) and Republic of Korea (15,279). USA numbers are relatively stable and low at 2,423, an increase of just 271 from 2014. The largest jump was in foreign students from Southeast Asia, of strategic interest to Japan in countering China's power, and expanding its national interest and security to the extended realm of East Asia. Vietnam (38,882), Nepal (16,250), and Myanmar (2,755) represent a 47%, 55%, and 42% respective increase in the total number of foreign students in Japan.

In my talks with foreign students in Japan, many do not feel well integrated into Japanese society. They may speak the language quite well, but they tell me that it is difficult to make friends with their Japanese fellow students. If I could make just one change to Japan's global outreach efforts, I would institute more pre-academic orientation programs that would allow foreign students in Japan to meet each other and form their own social and peer networks to increase their level of participation in Japanese society while here. These foreign students are incredible resources of understanding the world outside, but as is often the case, they are far too often taken for granted by their sponsoring institutions.

In Japan one's civic duties are not limited to paying taxes, lining up orderly to take the morning commute train, or separating one's trash for recycling. The Japanese people are more invested in their country's future than any arrow in the quiver of the leader of the Liberal Democratic Party. Who better than the people themselves to show the world who Japan is and what it is all about. So often the media coverage in Japan is a steady stream of Diet member comings and goings and reports about what Abe will say or do next. Not even corporate heads get the level of attention that Japanese politicians do, although this is more of a sign of the loss of Japan's top tier economic status and charismatic leadership in private industry.

2015, the anniversary year of the end of World War II, intensified "Abe 24," where we got wall-to-wall press coverage speculation about what Shinzo Abe might say on August 15, 2015, seventy years after Japan surrendered to Allied Forces in the Pacific. It made me wonder if NHK would produce a program called "The Mind of Abe," that would consist of reporters and analysts guessing at what is going on in his head before he says it. It might sound comical, but my point is serious: There is far too much coverage about politics in Japan that supersedes the stories of the people of Japan. This exaltation of politics and politicians in Japan is extreme. It leads to a condition where politicians think that they know better than the people whose interests they are supposed to serve, not the other way around.

Abe delivered his WWII primetime statement on Friday, August 14, 2015, one day before the official 70th anniversary. It pleased his domestic public enough to lift his favorability a few points, but displeased the rightist nationalists who were not happy with Japan's conceding to any aggression or remorse. For the far right in Japan, the country is always the victim, never the perpetrator. The speech predictably displeased the governments of South Korea and China."[67] Hua Chunying, spokesman for China's Foreign Ministry:

Japan should have made an explicit statement on the nature of the war of militarism and aggression and its responsibility on the wars, made sincere apology to the people of victim countries, and made a clean break with the past of militarist aggression, rather than being evasive on this major issue of principle.[68]

South Korean President Park Geun-hye said that the speech "left a lot to be desired" but was "notable" for supporting statements by past Japanese governments, leading some Japan watchers like Sheila Smith to say that Korea-Japan relations now had some "diplomatic wiggle room."[69] Whatever Abe said, he couldn't win over staunch opponents because it is his actions that speak louder than any words of contrition. Interestingly, he took an opportunity to reference women in his speech, but not comfort women specifically:

We will engrave in our hearts the past, when the dignity and honour of many women were severely injured during wars in the 20th century. Upon this reflection, Japan wishes to be a country always at the side of such women's injured hearts. Japan will lead the world in making the 21st century an era in which women's human rights are not infringed upon.[70]

Shannon Tiezzi in The Diplomat noted, "Park called for actions rather than words," and in "Seoul's standpoint, that particularly means 'a speedy and proper' resolution to the 'comfort women' issue."[71]

Abe said that future generations should not be expected to keep apologizing for past transgressions: "In Japan, the postwar generations now exceed eighty per cent of its population. We must not let our children, grandchildren, and even further generations to come, who have nothing to do with that war, be predestined to apologize."[72]

As I told the *Los Angeles Times*, "Words are fine, but what of the feeling behind them? Watch what he does, not always what he says. He's calling for future generations to be free of apology burdens. Well then, time to update the textbooks, not cleanse them of any wrongdoing. The world can move on when Japan fully accounts for its actions in documents of record."[73]

Months before Abe's suggestion that Japan avoid excessive apologies for a past not yet reconciled, a German foreign correspondent named Carsten Germis wrote a *sayonara* piece for the Foreign Correspondents' Club of Japan journal, *Number 1 Shimbun*. The title of the article grabbed eyeballs: "Confessions of a foreign correspondent after a half-decade of reporting from Tokyo to his German readers." It reached well beyond his German readers. It was a shot across the bow to warn global Japan watchers about the troubling Japanese government intervention of the free press (and by government in Japan nowadays we usually mean the LDP and its party head, Shinzo Abe).

The article was forwarded widely on social media and translated into Japanese because the source is credible. He is no wild-eyed soul who regularly harangues the powers that be. He writes for the German daily, *Frankfurter Allgemeine Zeitung*, a politically conservative and economically liberal (pro-capitalistic) newspaper like the *Wall Street Journal*. He's also not charged with being "FOB" (Fresh Off the Boat), a moniker used in this island nation to cut off anyone with whom you disagree in general or to silence someone who is considered particularly ignorant about Japanese ways and norms. The open letter from Germis reads like a rallying cry:

There is a growing gap between the perceptions of the Japanese elites and what is reported in the foreign media, and I worry that it could become a problem for journalists working here...there is a clear shift that is taking place under the leadership of Prime Minister Shinzo Abe – a move by the right to whitewash history. It could become a problem because Japan's new elites have a hard time dealing with opposing views or criticism, which is very likely to continue in the foreign media.

Carsten Germis could publish this critical opinion piece with less risk because he was leaving Japan. He would not have written such words were he trying to gain entry as a foreign correspondent to Japan. But he experienced a downturn in openness, a closing instead of an opening, at a time in Japan, just five years at that time before the 2020 Olympics, when it is trying very hard to present itself as open and ready for the world to come visit. His article compared his experience with the Democratic Party of Japan in contrast to the Liberal Democratic Party of Japan under Shinzo Abe. Whereas all three DPJ administrations (2010-2012) were open to explaining their positions to the foreign press, Abe's LDP is suspicious of any press criticism, particularly around the administration's revisionist wartime history views that are receiving a lot of drubbing in the foreign media. The LDP has all but disappeared from the FCCJ.

This lack of press access to power coincides with an official government to public diplomacy initiative through social media platforms Facebook and Twitter. What I call Abe 2.0 reflects a perception of more outreach on the part of the second administration of Abe that began in December 2012. The government message is to appear more transparent, but it's coming across as smoke and mirrors. Official communication efforts in Japan are predominantly one-way and centrally controlled. The increasing perception is that outliers should not participate, and if they do, they will be under greater scrutiny and pushback.

Undoubtedly Carsten Germis was pained to have to reveal that the country he knew a few years ago was no more. What he described is a country whose current political leadership is not just hypersensitive to press criticism–all governments react negatively to negative coverage–so that's to be expected. What got wide attention was his description of the amateurish behavior by the Ministry of Foreign Affairs to try to intimidate and discredit Germis through ad hominem attacks, i.e., he must, drumroll, please, be in the pocket of China. Germis writes:

> If this is an example of the government's beefed up global public relations, then we have cause to worry. Doesn't the Japanese consul general in Frankfurt have better things to do than worry about Chinese reprints?

This astonishing anecdote told by Germis reveals a media health problem. Asian studies scholar Jeff Kingston, my academic colleague at Temple University Japan, highlights three chronic conditions of Japan's malodorous communication 'illness' that lead to a repeat misdiagnosis of ramping up government paranoia and foreign press intimidation:

> The intolerance towards criticism is based on the erroneous belief that all criticism of Japanese government actions equals anti-Japanese sentiment. There is also a presumption that journalists are 'guests' who should be polite to their hosts while scholars who take Japanese research money also risk being labeled traitors if they express critical views. In 21st century Japan, there is far too much official paranoia that all criticism of Japan is aiding and abetting China and Korea. [74]

It's not just foreign reporters that are being singled out. There are scholars in Japan who are now being subjected to government pushback. Don't talk to so-and-so means anyone critical of the Abe regime. My friend and former Sophia University colleague, Koichi Nakano, holds a Ph.D. in political science from Princeton University. He's one of the most cited academics on Japan's politics but fell victim to a smear campaign to discredit him for being reliably critical of the Abe government. (To Nakano's credit, he has a lot of material to work with here.) Germis, among other foreign reporters, was told not to use Nakano as a source. And who told him? Press relations officials in the Abe administration!

To improve Japan's global reputation, the government of Japan must loosen its hold on the free press. Undue pressure on a press, whose duty is to report facts on the ground, creates more critics than defenders of Japan. A free and vibrant media system will report some good and bad news stories, but maintaining an open door policy between the government and the press will balance out the narrative.

Passive tolerance of dissent is not enough. The government of Japan should be proactive in its support for an independent, open, and vibrant foreign and domestic media system if it cares about how much a free press image impacts its nation brand image. And if Japan wants to expand its Cool Japan and Nice Japan global branding campaign, then muzzling the media is not how to go about it.

LAND OF THE RISING SISTER

Two decades ago when I first stepped foot on Japanese soil, I was a newly crowned female doctorate who was cautioned before my trip by my U.S. Government briefers not to use my credential title in Japan. Their rationale was that I was an outlier; very few Japanese women had an advanced degree, much less a Ph.D. I thought the request was odd since I wasn't Japanese and my having a Ph.D. as an American woman would be an opportunity for cross-cultural understanding of the role and standing of women in different societies. I would come to realize that the caution was designed to protect me from my sticking out too much in a culture where modesty, humility, and social etiquette are supreme virtues.

I noticed immediately that women in Japan were different from my grown up standard in America. First, these women had never experienced a women's movement like the second-wave feminist one we had in the United States that began at the time of the Civil Rights Movement of the 1960s and ended with the failure to ratify an Equal Rights Amendment (ERA) in 1982.[75] I knew about this feminism, Gloria Steinem, *Ms.* magazine and 'women's lib' as a child growing up in the 1970s. A favorite song was Helen Reddy's "I Am Woman," which I performed with a hairbrush microphone in the family den in front of my mom and a few household pets. I never doubted my capabilities living in a household of men with my parents, four older brothers and no sisters. The male to female ratio was 5:2. This male-centered environment taught me early on that I needed to make my voice heard above the din of the noise that four teenage boys can make, perform my best, and keep my eyes on the prize, whatever that prize may be. I wasn't limited to choosing family over a career. I could take the path of a career alone or pursue marriage, a family and a career. I had a choice because there were women and supportive men advocating for my freedom every day. Whatever fissures existed among feminists, ultimately the fight was for life choice and equality.

In contrast, Japanese society surprised me with its stark gender division. As a U.S. government official in foreign affairs, I was escorted around Japan's ministries and marveled at the sex segregation of the Japanese government office, including the Ministry of Economy, Trade, and Industry, Ministry of Defense, and Ministry of Foreign Affairs. Women were present, but they seemed more like decorative wallpaper. When a well-dressed attractive woman who appeared to be in her mid- to late 20s appeared with a pushcart to serve tea and coffee, I recall sarcastically whispering to a fellow U.S. Government official, "I bet she has a masters from Harvard." I do not recall meeting a female counterpart who briefed me on any policy-related matters. It was clear which gender was running the country. Throughout my three-week stay, women were disproportionately visible in jobs as translator, tour guide, coffee and teacart server, or secretary.

Women seemed to be in the background, quiet, helpful, but not in the foreground where the serious business occurred. It was almost as if they were being taken for granted. The women were highly educated, but our conversations often revolved around dating, marriage, and men, never careers. Some Japanese women spent social time with me and other international visitors at a camp near the base of Mt. Fuji. We learned how to make *origami* (folding paper) and *washi* (traditional paper). We laughed and splashed together in the *onsen* (Japanese bath) where I brought along my Japan mascot, "Dilly," a T-Rex mini-me version of Godzilla that I bought at a discount drugstore called Rodman's located near my Friendship Heights home in Washington, D.C. He is still with me today.

To be sure, I looked at my new environment with Western feminist eyes and sought out examples of sex-segregated conditions. I've learned since then to be more contextual and aware of my own cultural biases, but it looked like Japanese women were not just the second sex but also the second class. What I didn't tell myself then that I often remind myself now is that Japan's revitalization is completely dependent on the personal and political empowerment of women. Further, it cannot come from the top down inside the Prime

Minister's Office or the Diet (Japan's Parliament), but must come from the bottom up, by women, of women, and for women. The world's most famous cultural anthropologist, Margaret Mead, said, "Never depend upon institutions or government to solve any problem. All social movements are founded by, guided by, motivated and seen through by the passion of individuals."[76] Japan needs more than a media-hyped government moniker, Womenomics, concerned primarily with using women in the service of growth in GDP.[77] It needs a social movement with outspoken female role models who can galvanize the nation from the hinterland to Roppongi Hills.

My takeaway from my first trip in 1993 and a subsequent trip to Japan in 1994 convinced me that Japan was sidelining women, much to its detriment economically, but also globally. It just didn't make sense for what was then the world's second largest economy to be underutilizing such a well-educated, capable group of people who just happened to be female. I didn't view it as just patent sexism. Japan had become a super world economy by sex segregating societal roles. The public workplace was where men dominated and the private home domain was where women controlled the housework, childrearing, and family budget. It was a tradition in cultural norms and institutional mandate that was hard to overcome.

Shortly after my second trip to Japan in fall 1994, I conducted an interview with Masako "Miki" Kuriyama, the gracious wife of Takakazu Kuriyama, Japanese ambassador to the United States (1992-1995).[78] It was my first visit to the Japanese residence located near American University in Northwest Washington, D.C. Mrs. Kuriyama asked me if I were married and if I knew the parable of the Christmas cake. This was the first time I learned that Japanese women had an expiration date for marriage desirability, which in the mid-1990s, she jokingly said, had its 'shelf life' extended to end of December, a generous age of 31! These days I suppose one could freeze Christmas cake into January since some women here are putting off marriage or not marrying at all.

My initial exposure to Japan coincided with the country's economic slide when affirming women's added value in Japan's economy might have given it a much-needed boost. Why didn't it happen? One explanation offered by the Hofstede Centre in Finland is that Japan, notwithstanding the emasculation description of modern Japan by Nippon Kaigi, is a highly masculine society where competition among (presumably male-dominated) groups in industry, education, and politics is fierce. Cultural researcher Geert Hofstede says that Japan is "one of the most masculine societies in the world."[79] Masculine societies value competition, achievement and measurable success where success refers to a zero sum game of winner or best in class, which starts in grade school between sports teams and classrooms. Such a society is hierarchical in order to determine who is successful, according to rank and file. I liken Japan's high index in masculinity to a military imperial past, which still heavily influences Japanese ways today, even with the heritage of Japan's Article 9 that renounces war. We don't think of Japan as highly militaristic, but in this context, it is reflected in valuing masculine (male) tendencies over feminine (female) tendencies, where quality of life measures are also signs of success.[80] That high masculinity (strive to win and compete) permeates everywhere, even in the increasingly touted field of Japanese hospitality, which is now a focus in Japan's public diplomacy:

> …Masculinity in Japan is the drive for excellence and perfection in their material production (monozukuri) and in material services (hotels and restaurants) and presentation (gift wrapping and food presentation) in every aspect of life. Notorious Japanese workaholism is another expression of their masculinity. It is still hard for women to climb up the corporate ladders in Japan with their masculine norm of hard and long working hours.[81]

An example of this group competition orientation is exemplified in the centerpiece that the Japanese *meishi* (business cards) hold in personal exchange settings. The name card is so important to Japanese society that it has a website devoted to how to exchange meishi.[82] (It is considered a bit rude to show up to a networking event without your meishi and the preference is to stand and face the person with whom you are exchanging meishi.)

Meishi are less about the individual person and more about that individual's association to groups, be it academic, government or industry. If you give a name card with just your name and contact information but no institutional ties, you might get some puzzled looks. As an Abe Fellow, whenever I shared a meishi, the oohs and ahhs came from two affiliations, one as full professor at California State University, Fullerton and the other as a visiting professor and Abe Fellow at Keio University. The Abe logo hinted that I might be working with a certain Prime Minister Abe. I assured people that my Abe was "the other Abe," namely, Shintaro Abe, father of the prime minister, who had donated monies to the Japan Foundation to fund the Abe academic and journalism fellowships in his name.

All this talk about meishi relates to how women are viewed in Japanese society. For instance, women who work at home as homemakers don't require a name card the way an employed person does because domestic work is unpaid and hence, less valued. The homemaker affiliation is with the male spouse and family, which are not institutional but personal affiliations. Perhaps homemakers should have name cards and list all the work they do for no pay; maybe then it might occur to the politicians that GDP is not just a result of paid work, but rests on the shoulders of unpaid and underpaid people, mostly women, whose recognition is unappreciated.

Fast forward two decades after my first visit to Japan and Prime Minister Shinzo Abe's second term in office since his rather unremarkable first term (2006-2007) is public relations and buzzword friendly with a high degree of rhetorical emphasis on women's empowerment. Abe learned the hard way after his first term in office that how you roll out policy is similar to rolling out a new product. It must include marketing and media sophistication. Thus Abenomics was born. His Abenomics rollout consisted of three arrows—fiscal stimulus (e.g., raising the sales tax), monetary stimulus (e.g., weakening the yen), and systemic reform. In that last arrow, the toughest to hit its target so far, womenomics was born. In 2013, Abe made a formal declaration at the United Nations in New

York that he wanted to create a nation where all Japanese women can shine:

> There is a theory called 'womenomics,' which asserts that the more the advance of women in society is promoted, the higher the growth rate becomes. Creating an environment in which women find it comfortable to work and enhancing opportunities for women to work and to be active in society is no longer a matter of choice for Japan. It is instead a matter of the greatest urgency. Declaring my intention to create 'a society in which women shine,' I have been working to change Japan's domestic structures.

The nod to women's value was long overdue, especially since this is the same Abe who, as acting secretary-general of the Liberal Democratic Party in 2005, headed a campaign to quash a "gender-free" education movement that the LDP claimed would lead to "extreme" sex education instead of freeing men and women from fixed gender-specific roles.[83] In 2007, while still in his first term, Abe denied that so-called "comfort women" were anything but volunteers. He said, "there is no evidence to prove there was coercion," this, despite credible evidence and scholarship consensus that supports forced sexual enslavement.[84] In his second term in office, Abe once called for women to take a three-year absence from work after childbirth, which further demonstrated little understanding of working women's realities.[85]

As Abe noted in his *Wall Street Journal* op-ed, "Unleashing the Power of Womenomics,"[86] and subsequent UN speech, integrating Japanese women's power into the economy is a bottom line issue for Japan:

> We have set the goal of boosting women's workforce participation from the current 68% to 73% by the year 2020. Japanese women earn, on average, 30.2% less than men (compared with 20.1% in the U.S. and just 0.2% in the Philippines). We must bridge this equality gap.[87]

If fully utilized, women's participation in Japan's economy could increase gross domestic productivity (GDP) by as much as 13%.[88] I give Abe credit for bringing the highest level attention to the women's empowerment issue, but his showing up at women's conferences and giving women recognition in his speeches (including the 70th anniversary speech), alone isn't going to move the numbers unless women act on their own. Women in Japan are bereft of female role models. Younger women don't see their peers or older women in positions of political and economic power. Women make up 8-9% of the Diet, half the number of women in parliament in Saudi Arabia.[89] It's hard to imagine that the world's third largest economy and second largest advertising market would so devalue women in political participation.

I'm not one to question a policy change that is favorable to women's needs, but I would prefer a genuine women-directed movement where women get to decide on their own how they wish to shine. The womenomics spin-off to Abenomics is immersed in the patriarchal bottom line that still overworks all Japanese, mostly men now, but inclusively more women. Womenomics may inadvertently encourage women to overwork themselves just like their male counterparts. Other reforms are needed, including a more flexible work-life balance, which in workaholic Japan may be a long time coming.

Women in Japan today are caught in a bind. They are constantly bombarded with messages to join the workforce in greater numbers, and remain in or return to the workforce after marriage and childbearing. It must make many feel like they cannot possibly fulfill the wishes of their government, which is relying on their full participation in the workplace as well as their full participation as mothers. In Japan, only 63% of women participate in the workforce, and just 33% return to work after what is sometimes referred to as the 'lost' years, that period when women leave the paid workforce for unpaid work as wives and mothers. That leaves nearly 70% of women (two-thirds) who stop working altogether for at least a decade, compared to about 30% of American women. Many Japanese women who return to work after so many years will never return to a rank they held earlier. Many will end up in lower-paying, temporary, and non-career track jobs. Japanese men participate in the workforce at a rate of 85%. Paid full-time employment remains a masculine concept in Japan, especially full-time breadwinner, cradle-to-grave employment.

If I could sit down with Mr. Abe, I would say, "Mr. Prime Minister, women in Japan are already working. In fact, they have two jobs, one of which is unpaid. Women's work, and women in general, are underappreciated and undervalued." Women in Japan make between one third and one half the salary of their male counterparts. The Global Gender Gap Report 2015 reveals that women in Japan earn on average $24,389 compared to $40,000 for men.[90] Women's unpaid work at home adds up to 299 minutes per day (nearly 5 hours) versus 62 minutes for men. The ability of women to rise to positions of leadership power is under 4%. Seven out of ten Ph.D. graduates are male. Married women who work end up with two jobs, one paid, one unpaid, unless they can afford or find outside help. This disparity is explained in part by women's higher numbers in lower-paying professions and the fact that a third is engaged in part-time employment compared to a tenth of the male workforce.[91]

Japanese women are engaging in a new form of political participation, electing not to marry and have children so that they can pursue careers or a lifestyle that is affordable and allows more life/work balance. Perhaps Womenomics is a misnomer. It should be Balancenomics, Gendernomics. If women had greater participation in the workforce, more satisfying work assignments, and were helped by their male partners in unpaid work, then there might be an uptick in fertility rates. In places like Denmark and Sweden where women's employment is high, the birth rate is higher. In places like Korea and Italy where women's employment is low, the birth rate is much lower.

The Christmas cake scenario for women's ripeness for marriage is no more. Originally you were supposed to "throw out" the Christmas cake after the holiday. The mean age for marriage in Japan is now 30 years old and almost a third of Japanese women in their 30s has yet to marry. This is especially noticeable in urban sectors like Tokyo. In the U.S., women on average first marry by age 27. What I'm hearing from some of my Japanese women friends is that the stay-at-home mom with kids' scenario isn't appealing. The husband works all day, must entertain clients at night and returns home very late by train. He doesn't help around the house but expects his wife to take care of the children, his meals, his laundry, and everything else that his mother used to do for him. As his and her parents age, she too must step up to intervene. If Abenomics doesn't fully address policies that help women balance family and careers more successfully, women will become even less attracted to marriage and children.

Despite the research data and political rhetoric, in the World Economic Forum's Global Gender Gap Report 2015, Japan ranks 101st out of 145 countries, above Swaziland (102) and below Cyprus (100). The United States ranks 28th. In the category of high-income countries, only South Korea at rank 115 and a few Middle Eastern countries rank lower than Japan. Low- and middle-income countries ranked above Japan, including Azerbaijan (96) China (91) and the Russian Federation (75). On this scale, the higher the rank number, the worse the disparity between genders. Japan ranks first in gender equality in literacy, healthy life expectancy, and enrollment in secondary education. The low overall ranking is a result of women's poor political empowerment (104) and economic participation and opportunity (106).

The Japanese government likes to set target numbers that it often fails to deliver on. Those related to women are connected to the year 2020, like everything else. (You may have heard that Tokyo is hosting a Summer Olympics!) The Administration has pledged to increase the participation of women between the ages of 25 and 44 in the workforce to 73% by 2020, up from 68% in 2012. It also pledged to increase the percentage of women in leadership positions from 10% to 30%, although this figure was downgraded in December 2015 to more "realistic" goals from the wildly unattainable 30% to, in many respects, single digits.[92] For instance, the new goal percentage for ministry division directorships is 7%. Oops.

A couple of challenges connected to how many women in Japan want to take up leadership positions in Japanese companies involves the backlash from not just men but other women. Women may have to deal with resentment from other women as well as supervisory men in middle management who believe that these women jumped ranks or were promoted for affirmative action reasons only. The government cannot simply wave a magic wand and triple the number of women in executive management positions, especially if these women do not have the ambition or desire for these jobs or feel that they are not prepared to be fully accepted in the corner offices. Many women do not want to participate in the traditional Japanese work culture—excessively long work hours, at times very inefficient, followed by late night drinking sessions with their mostly male married and single coworkers.

In the U.S. we tend to separate our work life from our play or family life; the idea of going out drinking regularly with our co-workers is unappealing because many of us like to keep our off-work time private. If we do so, it is with people we choose. It is not a mandatory part of the job that seems to be the norm in Japan.

Japanese women have the longest life expectancy in the world at age 87, and yet I know a Japanese woman with a Ph.D. and MBA from Harvard who had to step down from her highest rank faculty appointment just because she turned 65. Women in academia in Japan have it almost harder than women in the corporate sector. Just three out of ten women in academia hold a doctorate compared to seven out of ten men. Women researchers are at the bottom of the food chain. Many are in part-time contract positions. They cannot advance in that career ladder. As of 2010, only 13.6 percent of university-level researchers were women. Naoko Ohri, herself a part-time lecturer at Hitotsubashi University in Tokyo, is co-author of *Kogakureki Joshi no Hinkon* (*The Poverty of Highly Educated Women*), which describes many elite universities in Japan as "gentlemen's clubs." As she says, "When women make up less than 20 percent of the workforce, it is extremely difficult for them to make a difference, to get their voices heard by the majority."[93]

We need to allow women to have lengthier productive work years instead of forcing retirement at arbitrary ages. The government of

Japan appointed a 65-year-old former minister to head the 2020 Olympics Committee. Political nepotism has its privileges.

In 1986 Japan passed the Equal Employment Opportunities Law, and yet today Japan sticks to a two-track system of hiring. One track is for elite-ranked specialized workers (*sogoshoku*); the other is for clerical and administrative support jobs (*ippanshoku*). In 2011, 11% of sogoshoku hires were women. Women are still viewed as potential baby makers who will leave the company for marriage and family. Too often Japanese companies do not wish to make that upfront investment in the female elite hires because they may 'jump ship' for maternity leave. A 2011 study conducted by the New York-based Center for Work-Life Policy found that college-educated Japanese women quit their jobs mostly because their career was not satisfying, and nearly half of them said that they felt actively stymied by their managers and work environment. Some of these women reported office bullying if they elect to return after having a child, what is called *matahara*, short for "maternity harassment."[94]

Politics in Japan remains a man's domain. Women are pushed to the front for window-dressing purposes, but by and large, women do not participate in numbers that make much difference. Further, young university-age women and men I know have no interest in participating in politics. If a woman has political ambitions, she might be shouted down for forcing herself into a man's world. In 2014, several male lawmakers in the Tokyo Metropolitan Assembly heckled a female politician during remarks she made at a hearing on maternity leave and infertility. They shouted, "Hurry up and get married!" and "Can't you give birth?"[95] Too often women in Japan are viewed as well served in the home or on their backs and knees in the pages of men's magazines and risqué manga.

We cannot view women's participation in Japanese society as a narrow economics issue. It is a human rights and human dignity issue. If you learn to treat women with more respect, value, and personal agency, you'll see them not only want to work more, but with more ambition, and with more willingness to marry and have children for the good of this society. If the overall attitude toward women in Japan remains sexualized, marginalized and ancillary to the whole, then don't expect women to answer the call of the prime minister that women should shine. And yet, change is afoot.

On June 29, 2015, I attended the third annual summit of Women in Business in Tokyo. Sponsored by the American Chamber of Commerce in Japan, this year's gathering peaked at 700 women and men in attendance, up from a few hundred women in 2013. There is something in the air when both the prime minister and ambassador of the United States return for a second year to reinforce their commitment to raising the level of women's visibility in politics and business. Abe's participation in many women's conferences throughout Japan is a positive sign of change, but it's not enough. I can't read Abe's heart or mind and would like to give him the benefit of the doubt, but his women-friendly rhetoric doesn't seem to be coming from a place of altruism or feminism. More Japanese women working and more of these same women rising to executive leadership positions in Japan is viewed as an economic necessity, not a feminist gender-equality manifesto.

If Japan were a stronger economy, it is highly doubtful that its prime minister would be championing women working more outside the home because Japan's modern growth has been built on a sharp division of labor between the Japanese salaryman working and commuting excessively long hours while women control the family income, childrearing, and domestic duties inside the home. What's different today is that more Japanese women I meet, or at least those working in the larger urban sectors, are increasingly working professionals who may delay marriage and children or never marry in order to have a more luxurious lifestyle. I can't say as I blame them since I too am an urban-based professional unmarried woman with no children.

Nevertheless, Abe's vision for women in Japan is a long overdue recognition that the nation formerly known as No. 1 (Ezra Vogel's 1979 classic, *Japan As No. 1*) is, since 2011, the number three global economy in GDP and slipping downward due to its enormous public debt, which is twice its annual gross domestic product, the worst of any leading industrialized economy in the world. According to a 2011 World Bank study on the purchasing power parity of leading economies, India is now ahead of Japan, not a favorable position for Japan since the number 4 is pronounced "shi" (shee) in Japanese, the same sound for death.

Regardless of my gripes about Prime Minister Abe's purist intentions, he must be applauded for placing women and the Japanese economy on equal footing. I do notice the lack of both positive and powerful female role models in Japanese society. When one lives in Japan, you see Japanese women on constant display in commercial advertising, as pop idols, anime fantasy girlfriends, and in pornography, including the men's magazines on display at the convenience store. Occasionally you may see a career woman in advertising, but not enough. You can turn on cable television and see a bit of soft porn with your morning coffee, often an underage woman sitting in underwear in a bathtub licking on a Popsicle. This isn't the image of Japan that Womenomics has in mind with the oft-cited goal of reaching greater representation in top management by 2020.

In real life, Japanese women are the backbone of lower paying non-career track jobs (*hiseiki*), accounting for "up to 70 percent of the nation's part-time or non-permanent workforce, receiving less pay, benefits and job security than their full-time counterparts."[96] This is not to say that there aren't professional women role models at all, but their numbers are still insignificant. It's more common in Japan that a foreign woman will model women's advancement, especially in the corporate or diplomatic sector, than a Japanese woman.

At the growing circuit of women's conferences I attend in Tokyo, one tends to see a lot of the same Japanese women present as speakers, including Japanese-American woman Kathy Matsui of Goldman Sachs, Yoko Ishikura of the World Economic Forum and Davos Experience in Tokyo (DEX) or Mayor Fumiko Hayashi of Yokohama. All of these women I respect and admire immensely, but when you see a lot of the same women leaders and know their biographies, you might conclude that women's leadership in Japan is for an exclusive club with few spaces open to newcomers. It's important to widen the lens of one's leadership periscope and include faces that aren't so often seen on the women's speaking circuit.

Inside academia, women are most often seen in administration or support staff levels, but not in roles as researchers or *kyoju* (professor.) A Japanese university may have female faculty, but on average fewer than one out of five of a Japanese female student's professors will be female, while four out of five will be male, a ratio of 4 to 1 that reinforces where power, influence and authority naturally reside in a workplace environment. It's even harder to picture women as university academics and researchers, a situation one Kyoto professor describes as "backward" in comparison to Japan's global counterparts:

> When compared to other OECD (Organization for Economic Cooperation and Development) countries, the situation of female academics and scientists in Japan has often been described as being backward. As of 2013, there were 127,800 female and 759,200 male researchers in Japan. The percentage of women among all researchers in Japan has been gradually increasing, but still stands at 14.4%, whereas the corresponding rates in OECD countries are estimated to be two to three times higher than that of Japan.[97]

In my field of social science (political science/international relations), women faculty in Japan represent 23% of the overall faculty, while women account for just 9% of university researchers in engineering and just 13% in the natural sciences. As one moves up the academic ranks, women's presence declines. While Japanese women make up half of junior college faculty where 90% of the student body is female, they are in a distinct minority at the highest university rank of full professor, just 13% in the social sciences (e.g., economics, political science, international relations, geography, sociology). Women's visibility at all ranks is best in nursing, education, health and home economics.

U.S. Ambassador to Japan Caroline Kennedy's remarks at the 2015 ACCJ Women in Business Summit were particularly salient given her mythical history as John F. Kennedy's sole remaining living heir. As a lawyer, mother, author, speaker, and most important, the U.S. Government's top diplomat in Tokyo, Caroline Kennedy has become her own agent for change around the issue of women's empowerment in Japan. Despite facing death threats,[98] Kennedy has remained highly visible in her dedication to the empowerment of women in Japan. As she rightly notes, there is no more urgent or important factor in the long-term profitability of Japanese companies and the Japanese economy than the full and fair participation of women.

It's hard to believe that such a wealthy, highly educated nation like Japan, a country so admired for its postwar perseverance and dedication to rebuilding itself as a market economy, with its high standard of living and world renowned work ethic, would have intentionally left out half of its population from the highest levels of decision-making, research, and management, but intentional or not, that's exactly what has happened.

We cannot overlook the fact that Japan was and remains a patriarchal nation. Women have historically had to make the toughest decisions in this society at three times: marriage, childbirth, and when their last child (increasingly only child) starts school and is no longer at home full-time.[99] This leaves a lot of the everyday management of other tough decision in politics and economics in men's hands. It wasn't too long ago that Kumiko Hashimoto, the wife of the 82nd and 83rd Prime Minister of Japan, Ryutaro Hashimoto (1996-1998) said, "I don't interfere with my husband's business, not with my mouth, hands or legs."[100]

To add a twist to this plea to make Japanese women the center of the universe in Japan, to a large extent, they already are. Women dominate advertising in Japan. Marketers study Japanese women for their style and taste preferences. Walk the streets of Tokyo and you will see countless Japanese women, who, from head to toe, are the picture of elegance and sophistication. Japanese women are considered some of the most gracious, polite and refine women in the world. It is a stereotype, but it's a positive one. They are an Asian equivalent to the French cool.[101] They create trends in fashion, food and style that catch the interest of global marketers and cultural creatives. Pop icon Gwen Stefani built a fashion and music empire on the Harajuku girls roaming Takeshita Dori. Japanese women travel the world and engage in study abroad far more than their male counterparts. In marriage, Japanese women traditionally control the home, its finances, childcare, and even child custody after divorce or separation. Japanese women are increasingly electing to put off marriage and children or never marrying at all. In person, I am struck at the cultural gap between real Japanese women and the giggly, submissive, pleasing doe-eyed automaton version of Japanese women that appears in a lot of popular culture.

Don't be fooled by media versions that coat your eyes about what to expect from Japanese women. They are strong, getting stronger, and they will save Japan in the 21st century. Where they don't show up enough is in politics and industry, and to a large extent in the academy. Japanese women are soft power wonders in commercial and cultural venues, but not in political and economic venues. This will change. It has to.

A CULTURAL CREATIVE SUPERPOWER

Culture drives Japan's diplomatic relations. At times it can open doors, as in the ill-named and unstrategic "Cool Japan" program. But equally so, Japan's culture closes doors to the world because to some, if you are not an expert on Japan or speak the language, you are often deemed outside the inner circle of "the knowing."

My target audience of readers for this book is not the Japan expert but the Japan interested, the Japan curious, regardless of one's Japanese language ability.

Japanologists are often a prickly lot in that they pride themselves on their in-depth knowledge of both culture and language. Both Japanese culture and the Japanese language are seen as almost impenetrable to anyone but those who spend their lives in study or have worked for many years in Japan. This is why it is so common to be asked how long you've been in Japan. Your place in the pecking order of 'ability to judge' is fixed by length of time in country. Newer observers of Japan are often dismissed as just not knowing enough about Japan to comment on it. So let me make myself perfectly clear: I am not trying to challenge those who have the competitive edge in language and culture. I'll never catch up with you so why keep running. I'd rather take the non-expert and the Japan curious on a leisurely stroll through closer inspection of Japan's culture and how it relates to foreign policy.

My goal is to bring more people into conversations about Japan so that Japan becomes a more interesting subject, not only to foreigners near and far, but also to the Japanese people. I'm reminded by what a Japanese diplomat said in a *New York Times*' front-page article to explain why his country is beefing up its efforts to influence Washington: "Japan is not necessarily the most interesting subject." I'm sure that he said much more than that, but as reported, it made Japan sound like it had a serious case of the Eeyore, the down in the dumps donkey friend of Winnie the Pooh. I suppose that's what twenty years of headlines about the "lost decades" can do to a country's libido.

A few Japanese have shared with me a sense that Japan's best days are behind it, that it is a dying society—despite having the highest percentage of centurions. They tell me that other neighboring countries like China, Korea, and Taiwan matter more to the world than Japan. I don't agree that Japan's best days are behind it or I wouldn't have bothered publishing this collection of observational essays. With a little encouragement, the Japanese people can realize their full potential in international relations, particularly at the interpersonal level.

We often associate Japan with high tech rice cookers and toilets, virtual girlfriends, electronics, robotics, and *emoji* (emotional icons), and yes, Pokemon Go, but the true strength of Japan is real people with their real emotions, feelings, thoughts and opinions. When you get beyond the veneer of a highly developed, materialistic society, you find the core of human relations: We're all trying to make better sense about ourselves and our relations to others.

Having grown up in the Deep South of the United States with a childhood fueled by singing in the church choir and listening to a Sunday preacher, I fancy myself a bit of a cultural missionary on a diplomatic mission to invite non-experts on Japan or even just the passersby to feel connected to Japan and the Japanese people. There is no reason for non-Japanese speaking people to feel that they just have to move on to more open and accessible cultures. Call my effort a democratization of Japan's place in the world. I'm making an attempt to open the door to greater mutual understanding between Japanese people and their counterparts overseas. In order to do this, it all begins with Japanese culture and communication, and in extension, cross-cultural understanding. There is no other way.

One of the best books I've found on the subject of Japanese culture is *The Japanese Mind* by editors Roger Davies and Osamu Ikeno.[102] This collection of essays does not presume expertise on Japan but invites the reader to take a journey with insights from senior seminar students in cross-cultural communication at Ehime University. The first subject presented in understanding the Japanese mentality is ambiguity or *aimai*. I couldn't agree more. Japanese people learn to live with a lot of ambiguity without the usual angst that a Westerner would feel in communication. In intercultural communication literature by Edward Hall and others, we call this manner of ambiguity and indirectness a high-context culture. It's no coincidence that the cover of Edward Hall's *Beyond Culture* book has a painting of a traditional Japanese woman in kimono and hair chopsticks with a Hollywood sign mask across her eyes.[103]

Japan is one of the world's greatest high-context cultures, with the emphasis on great. You can spend your life trying to figure out the ins and outs of what is really meant, but that's part of the puzzle that makes living here so exciting. And because a high-context culture puts a lot of emphasis on nonverbal communication, you can maneuver your way through gestures and behavior to make sense of otherwise confusing scenarios. That does not always mean that there aren't hurdles. A non-Japanese person, even one who knows the language, may never fully embrace the entire meaning.

A New Zealand-born, Japan-residing friend of mine, Cole Cameron, describes this high tolerance for ambiguity as functioning like a personal WiFi:

In my years of experience living and working among the Japanese, I learned that Japanese people communicate often through personal WiFi invisible antennas facilitating near field non-verbal and non-visual communication-that at first can be mystifying to non-Japanese. Over time I developed a deeper understanding of this and discovered the Japanese term *ishin-denshin*. It's an idiom defining a form of communication through unspoken mutual understanding. In English we can roughly translate ishin-denshin as "tacit understanding."

Adding another layer of complication when there is verbal communication is the Japanese term *haragei*, which roughly means communicating real intention through implication. It's up to the receiver of the message to put two-and-two together. As you can imagine, for someone raised in a low-context culture, these two characteristics--mystical "wireless message exchanges" and vague implications--of the high-context Japanese culture can be difficult to grasp, or at the very least accept that they exist. At face value it is easy to feel sometimes that Japanese people are underhanded in their dealings, more particularly in a business situation, because things happen and people's thoughts magically align as if there was a pre-meeting or a memo circulated beforehand which you were not privy to.[104]

This comfort with ambiguity might be the result of Japan's rice-growing society. Growing rice is an arduous process that requires a lot of group cooperation and interdependency with a focus on working together harmoniously for greater good. If people are too explicit and direct in their communication, conflict more easily occurs and the rice cultivation task is threatened. Whereas rice is often understood as a point of contention in trade talks—the United States endlessly lobbies for Japan to open up its rice market, rice is best understood as deeply embedded in the philosophy of how people communicate in Japan (see also my essay about Ise Jingu). In modern Japan, just a small percentage of people are still involved in rice production and many foreign workers have now replaced villagers in cultivation. Nevertheless, rice is everywhere in the landscape of Japan, from *onigiri* at the *conbini*, to a meal staple. The omnipresence of rice in Japan even figures into language. *Gohan,* the word for meal, also refers to cooked rice.[105]

Today, "fancy" rice cookers, along with high-tech toilets, are some of the hottest "Designed in Japan" items among the ever-growing number of wealthier tourists. Some rice cookers range from $400 to $1,000 and include smartphone compatibility.[106] Japan would do itself a lot of promotional good if it created personal stories to include with these rice cookers, a way to bridge the cultural divides and tensions that permeate the region.

In 2012, the Silicon Valley-based computer software company Adobe Systems published a survey about place branded creativity. Called "State of Create," the study revealed what people living in the world's leading economies of France, Germany, Japan, the United Kingdom and the United States thought about where the most creative places among them were located.

Every country besides Japan declared Japan the most creative nation and Tokyo the most creative city. Japanese respondents chose the United States as the most creative country and New York City as the top creative city. What gives?

The explanation was that Japan tends to associate creativity with an industry or specialized community known as "The Arts." In the Adobe survey, nearly eight out of ten Japanese surveyed agreed with the statement that "being creative is still reserved for the arts community," the only country to show such a large majority opinion. A sushi chef can be creative as can a painter or a musician, but many Japanese do not view themselves as personally creative unless they are in the creative industries.

So it sounds like in Japan to be creative one must create something tangible (music, a landscape picture, thinly sliced fish on rice), but not necessarily think creatively in general. There is no payoff to creatively thinking for oneself if one cannot mesh well in the team or group. In fact, it can be seen as detrimental to one's societal advancement. In contrast, ask an American about personal creativity and most would say, "Heck yeah, I'm creative!"

I've been told many times by natives and foreigners with years of experience living in Japan that the educational system in Japan does not place a strong emphasis on students' individual creative impulses. In part it is due to the preponderance of time spent in preparing for national examinations that will determine how far and where a student's higher education will continue. A Japanese friend who spent most of her adult life overseas said that in learning how to draw the correct Kanji as a child she had to carefully keep the pen strokes inside the box. The perfect stroke was emphasized. Do it the same each time. In other words, perhaps there isn't enough time spent coloring outside the lines or thinking outside the box. Maybe that is allowed to come later in life, not on a young person's path of preparation for economic productivity. Rote memorization in one's school subjects is common in Japan, even in literature classes where the Great Works are largely interpreted by the *Sensei*, not the students. English as a second language is taught by native Japanese-speaking teachers with often foreign-born assistant language teachers from the JET program. Further, English is taught as a set of grammar rules and vocabulary in preparation for multiple-choice tests. Little, if any, time is set aside for creative exchange of thoughts and ideas in the adopted language, an activity that might actually make the English learning lessons quite fun and relaxing. This leads to the common predicament of Japanese students of English as a Second Language feeling shy and quiet about speaking English.

I experienced this lack of creative exchange of ideas in conversation play out at one of Japan's top private universities. Sophia University has a well-deserved reputation for having Japanese students with a much higher command of English. My students were smart and capable learners and had a good command of English in writing. But I found some were insufficiently prepared to verbally communicate in English because they were a product of a secondary school system that emphasized written over oral mastery of the language. I was encouraged to write my discussion questions on the board for the students to answer in written memos that I would collect in class. From that pool, I would pick out the best answers, being careful not to single out a student, but rather commenting, "One student gave the following answer."

In his book, *Creativity: Flow and the Psychology of Discovery and Invention*, Mihaly Csikszentmihalyi, Director of the Quality of Life Research Center at Claremont Graduate University, identifies a creative individual as paradoxical—energetic, but in need of quiet and rest; smart and naïve; playful and disciplined; responsible and irresponsible; rebellious and independent; passionate but also objective; imaginative and fantasy-oriented at times and rooted in reality at other times: extroverted and introverted; humble and proud; exist outside rigid gender roles and may even lean toward androgyny. "The openness and sensitivity of creative individuals often exposes them to suffering pain yet also a great deal of enjoyment."[107]

Given Japan's anime and manga industry and its fan base otaku culture full of cosplay, its multi-subcultures in sex, age, occupation, relationship status, region, and education, one could very well use these individual creative attributes to project onto Japan. This explains why outsider eyes see Japan as so creative, but it doesn't explain why the Japanese tend to segment creative personalities by pursuit and thereby downplay their creative juices.

A government agency with a most uncreative name may hold some answers. The Institute of Statistical Mathematics has been conducting a time series on Japanese self-images since the postwar years to the present. The findings are quite stunning. Despite all the changes in Japanese society from the immediate post-Occupation period to the 21st Century, Japanese assessment of their values and images has remained remarkably consistent. Over six decades (1958-2008),[108] Japanese have recorded themselves highly on the following four characteristics, that is, with a slight to strong majority: diligent; courteous; kind; persevering.

Japanese regard themselves as only slightly idealistic, with a high mark of one out of three (32%) in 1958 and a low mark of one out of five (20%) in the 2000s. In 1958, 23% of Japanese identified with cheerful, which dropped to 14% by 1963.

Among the following four characteristics, rational, liberal, easygoing, and creative, Japanese barely get into double digits. The worst among the four was creative. Across seven decades, only two times did creative reach a double digit. In 1983, 11% of Japanese identified themselves as creative and in 1988, 10%. All other years were 7-9%.

When I asked a Japanese friend to explain what seemed from my Western, US-origin eyes to be low self-esteem around creativity, she said that it's not so much individual, but collective. It is the proverbial "nail that sticks out must be hammered down" syndrome, but that's just one possibility. In a societal sense, being creative in Japan is associated with being outside the norm, exactly what many around the world view in a refreshing sense as creative in both ideas and imagination. But a Japanese person who falls too far outside accepted parameters suffers possible social isolation and may also be seen as less economically productive, what seems to be an original sin. This may explain why the artists I've met in Japan are often living on the margins of existence, unless they are able to secure an outside sponsor, which is very hard to come by unless you are extremely young, malleable, and capable of the right repackaging for the consumer market. Living for one's art for art's sake may be creative but will also lead to poverty. Is this why self-described diligent Japanese associate creativity so often with just the arts and not with their individual hearts and minds? Foreign eyes see creative Japan. Why can't Japan?

BRAND JAPAN: PAST, PRESENT, FUTURE

A battered, war-torn history pervades the Northeast Asian region and permeates the subjective memory of a growing chorus of antagonists, whether in China, Japan or Korea, who cannot see beyond images of a fictional "other," an amorphous being with whom one has little perceived common experience or values.

Seventy years have passed since the end of Japan's inglorious defeat as an imperial war power. A prideful government led by Shinzo Abe has stepped forward to reclaim Japan's glorious past and restore a sense of patriotism. This effort is testing Japan's global image from that of a pacifist postwar nation that forever renounced the use of force in resolving disputes to that of an assertive military regime that will shift its Self Defense Forces to a collective defense on offense alert. This may include intervening in overseas national conflicts or coming to the assistance of the world's leading military power, the United States of America. But do the nationalistic, prideful ends justify these hard power means? The Japanese public is most assuredly against such a twist in its national narrative. Self-defense is a good option, allowing one to stay out of a lot of the world's trouble spots, and pacifism is as calming as a rural onsen. Why ruin a good thing—the Japanese Constitution, specifically Article 9--that was born from such misery and destruction? A lot of the push for political change comes from the personal will of Abe.

Prime Minister Shinzo Abe is the son of the longest serving foreign minister in Japan's history, Shintaro Abe, but it is the maternal grandfather, Nobusuke Kishi, who preoccupies the attention and memory, dare I say, even obsession, of the current prime minister. Kishi, appointed Minister of Munitions by Prime Minister Hideki Tojo, was designated a "Class A" war criminal suspect and imprisoned at the end of World War II for supporting the defeated imperial government. He was released without indictment or trial. Once Japan came out of the Occupied Era in 1952, Kishi rose in political ranks to become Japan's 56th and 57th Prime Minister. He worked closely with the victorious postwar

American occupiers to pass a hotly contested security treaty in 1960 that brought out the largest number of demonstrators in Japanese history, forcing his resignation. If one were to provide a psychological analysis of today's prime minister, the grandson of Kishi, it is the shadow memory of the Sugamo Prison where his grandfather sat accused of war crimes that preoccupies the mind of Shinzo Abe.

In April 2015, Mr. and Mrs. Abe visited the United States. Viewed through the prism of the stateside media coverage, the trip seemed to have been a very successful personal mission, dubbed "Abe's excellent adventure," by The National Interest.[109] "By any measure, Japanese Prime Minister Shinzo Abe's visit to the United States has been a resounding success," crowed Michael Auslin in the conservative weekly, National Review.[110] Auslin, who attended several Abe events in Washington, was obviously wooed by the prime minister's "smile diplomacy,"[111] which convinced me that Auslin doesn't spend much time in Tokyo, where Abe is seen frowning at his opponents or street protesters as often as he's seen smiling!

Nevertheless, there is no question that Abe's trip to the East and West Coast of America reinforced to the American audience that Japan is back, that Japan is America's "willing" ally, and that postwar Japan and the United States are tied to each other like a child's umbilical cord attaches to the mother. The U.S.-Japan Joint Vision Statement released during Abe's visit reinforced this congenital attachment but stepped up that vision to announce an end to Japan's pacifist tradition of the past seventy years and the likelihood of joint military exercises, albeit framed in deterrence and defense rhetoric.[112] Abe's successful spring trip reminded Americans that Japan stands today, seventy years after the end of World War II, as one of America's closest allies in the world and arguably its closest ally in Asia.

As I watched the media coverage from my Tokyo apartment of Abe's excellent adventure to the United States (April 26-May 3, 2015), and read all the tweets that elevated his trip to a Rock 'n' Roll Tour (#AbeInTheUSA), I couldn't help but think about how far these two nations have come from being fierce enemies driven to so much death and destruction. I'm the daughter of a 20-year-old Navy ensign who served aboard the USS Missouri (BB-63) eight months after Japan's formal signed surrender aboard the battleship. The close relations between the United States and Japan today are nothing short of a marvel. Nevertheless, Japan needs to step outside of the U.S. shadow. It can do that by telling its own stories to the world, distinct and separate from its bilateral relations.

Japan is already a brand in itself. It is recognized for high quality dedication, precision and presentation. Is it necessary to further continue branding Japan, given that there is already such a positive image of Japan in the world? For many Japanese who value modesty, promoting oneself is not appreciated.

I'd like to challenge this conventional wisdom that Japan's cultural DNA orientation to modesty limits country promotion. You answer the call of promotion every day. What's the world's largest media market? It's the U.S. The second is Japan. What's the world's top media and entertainment capital? It's New York. Tokyo, Japan is the second largest entertainment & media spending market on the planet. Yes, the planet. Tokyo was the number one E&M sector until 2014 when New York edged it out ($19.7B to $19.5B). Advertising is all about promotion. It's in your face here. Picture Shibuya, Shinjuku, the Tokyo Metro, where one can bump one's head on advertising banners. Everywhere you look, products are being promoted. Even how products are wrapped and presented is promotion.

Japan is just as obsessed with its reputation as any other place, but it's more polite to not want to admit to promotion. Where Japan differs from the U.S. is that we in the U.S. celebrate self-promotion and we do not consider it a negative thing. We put emphasis on speaking up and letting people know who you are and what you can do. Where Japan diverges is in the public/private self (loosely translated, though more complex, as *tatamae/honne*). Personal branding is more novel in Japan, not nonexistent, but frowned upon more than institutional branding. The government of Japan promotes itself endlessly; nationalists make themselves heard; big business does the same. Nothing screams promotion more than the 51-story Dentsu Tower of Japan's dominant domestic advertiser and the Top 5 global advertiser. Japan needs to be frank that it embraces promotion. It's endemic to our way of life in modern global digital society. Even Facebook is becoming primarily a timeline of personal promotion.

That said, we must distinguish between branding and nation branding Japan. Branding in Japan refers mostly to promotion of goods and services, and foreign luxury brands are the most common pictures that come to mind (Kate Spade, Michael Kors, Gucci). What needs attention is the awareness importance of nation brand Japan— the overall good name and reputation of the country, people, and culture of Japan in the world that contributes to Japan's leadership in a competitive global economy.

Let's start with the obvious. It is a key player in global trade and now, with a weakened yen in the last several years, is becoming overrun with tourists from the region (China, Taiwan, S. Korea). It has a vested interest in increasing its exports and promoting more foreign direct investment and venture capital. It cannot afford to avoid branding itself. It brands itself like any other country just by being recognized globally as one of the world's top economies, the Economic Miracle of the 60s to the 1980s., and even today one of the top three global economies with the U.S. and China. The problem for Japan is that Japan is playing catch-up in building its reputation in the region. China and Korea are further along in nation branding. That doesn't mean that all is golden. China's Confucius Institutes, established in 2004, are expected to increase to 1,000 by 2020. They are receiving pushback from some host countries, including the U.S., which are questioning the propaganda nature of these language and culture centers. Sometimes spending too much on nation branding can backfire, but also spending too little.

South Korea has its own approach with its King Sejong Institute and Korean Cultural Centers. Right here in Tokyo in Yotsuya, the headquarters of the Japan Foundation is a minute away from the Korean Cultural Center. This Center is one of 29 Korean Cultural Centers in 24 countries. The Japan Foundation celebrated its 40th anniversary in 2012. It has 24 overseas branch offices in 23 countries.[113] When Abe came into office in December 2012, Japan's public diplomacy budget had been on a decade-long decline, cut by one-third. Abe vowed to improve the image of "beautiful" Japan in the world. Since then, the public diplomacy global charm offensive has subsequently increased, mostly through the launch of METI's Cool Japan Fund in late 2013 and global PR efforts like the announcement of Japan House in 2015.

What makes Brand Japan unique from other countries like Korea and China? Japan stands out in its *Kawaii* cute culture that has become a cultural stereotype, especially attached to both girls' and women's sensibilities. (In other words, Kawaii has no age expiration!) Japan is also associated with the *Otaku* geek, ueber-enthusiast culture exemplified by anime (animation) and manga (comic books), but even those Japan origin platforms are going global naturally on their own with American companies like Netflix, Amazon Prime and Hulu opening up Tokyo offices for foreign direct investment. The Japanese government doesn't need to promote these industries globally. What concerns the government fundamentally is maintaining a pure image of Japan as a perfection brand in education, service, language, and society presentation. Being well-mannered is automatic. There is more formality and politeness on the surface of the culture that extends to the foreign impression of the place. Newcomers to Japan comment on how nice and clean Japan is, how polite the people are, generally quiet and well-behaved. Being too loud is considered extremely rude. The manner of dress in the large urban areas, where most foreigners congregate, is well put together from head to toe. This sleek, albeit, often monochrome dress, inspired an idea for a global communications company I call The Nines. It is based on the expression, "To the Nines" as in "to a great or elaborate extent, to the highest degree, perfection." The women in Japan are often dressed to the nines. This Japanese female archetype is so well presented, immaculate, and sophisticated that its gender brand has become world-renowned.

Paradoxically, Japan tends to undervalue its global communication abilities and overvalue its exclusivity. The two-edged

Samurai sword about Japan is "uniqueness" of culture, that Japan is like no other place in the world. For example, BBC reporter Anita Rani opened the 2013 documentary, "No Sex Please, We're Japanese" with this: "The world's population is seven billion people and counting, and when you come to Tokyo, it feels like most of them live here. *But Japan is so different from any country in the world* (my emphasis). Men and women are drifting apart." It isn't just her opinion, but many Japanese would probably share the same point of view.

Yes, Japanese culture is different, but there are commonalities with what an international visitor enjoys and expects, notably safety, convenience, high standards in cuisine, accommodation, and public transportation. It's not too unique to be explored and appreciated. If I had *ichi-man* for every time I heard a comment along the lines of "You'll never truly know Japan," I would be a very rich woman indeed. Japan is knowable enough, both in culture and language, the latter being my struggle. I would not bother transferring my livelihood from Southern California to Japan if I did not believe that I had a purpose here as a global citizen with deep affection and admiration for Japanese society, warts and all.

A Japanese moral value that could be applied universally and marketed better in the world is this: loyalty to commitments, a working will to serve, even at personal sacrifice. It is based on a Japanese interpretation of Confucian values. Japanese values espouse social harmony, a public self that is mindful of how one's actions impact others, which I might reconfigure—with my Christian educational background–as The Golden Rule. Most of the literature on Japanese morals states that absolutist black/white rules of behavior are less salient here than a relativistic ethic based on the situation. You behave and speak appropriately as the situation demands.

To call Japan a monolithic homogenous culture is true, but misleading. There exists an internal multicultural society based on a dominant formal system structure with a lot of subcultures in work and play. The rigid rules orientation is what can make Japan seem a bit moralizing to the outsider who inevitably will make mistakes and violations to the social order. The imported philosophy of Confucianism dominates everyday life—preserving social order and advancing on merit.

Because Japanese see themselves primarily through group affiliations (university, workplace, family, ancestral village), intragroup and intergroup relationships take precedence above individual preference. When brands are promoted in Japan, they are often designed to get the person to fit in more, not to distinguish oneself outside. Likewise, ethics are often defined in Japan as more relativistic and situational than universal or particularistic. The members of any Japanese group linked by a web of mutual obligations are apt to forget their manners when they have to deal with unrelated, ill-placed groups, i.e., the *gaikokujin* (informal, *gaijin*), or "outside person." This sets off a tendency to communicate less successfully with non-Japanese. Many Japanese can be diffident, exhibiting modesty and shyness from lack of confidence. The lack of global communicative response comes from a genuine perplexity at how to deal with foreigners who are by definition outside the native web of commitments.

The solution is that Japan needs to better utilize its foreign resident community, both non-Japanese speakers and Japanese speakers. Foreigners are in Japan for various reasons: to study Japanese, because of their job, for a short-term degree program (cultural/educational exchange). We cannot presume that every foreigner wants to promote the Japan brand. There are plenty of foreigners already promoting Japan in the world, but there is a tendency for native Japanese to think that only natives can best represent the true nature of Japan. That works very well internally but not very well externally. I deal with the external environment. The Cool Japan Fund, for instance, is run almost entirely by Japanese bureaucrats, in concert with their comfortable business partners, and the grants favor Japanese legacy companies. Likewise, the Japanese Olympic Committee executives are all Japanese but the Olympics movement and organization are global entities. Branding Japan in the world is a global endeavor. You need global input. Stacking a board with all natives is the norm in a high context, consensus-driven work environment, but this doesn't translate into success when the global media and global public opinion drivers like social media are weighing in on and judging Japan's every move. Be careful what you wish for—the whole world is watching and it will continue to watch as we get closer to 2020.

2016 is a global agenda year and perfect time to recharge Japan's leadership role in the world. 2016 is the 60th anniversary of Japan's membership in the United Nations. As of January 1, 2016, Japan sits on the United Nations Security Council for a record 11th time as a temporary member. It's an opportunity for Japan to exhibit its leading cultural economy indicators in health and wellness, longevity, and in sustainability messages, as it emphasized this year at the G7 Summit in Ise-Shima. In terms of explaining Japan's global agenda to the world, Japan has not been very successful. It's much better at promoting Japanese products—particularly popular and trendy things.

Japan's main problem is its loss of global translators, synthesizers, storytellers and reporters in country and operating as a thriving, lively and engaged foreign press presence. The Foreign Press Center of Japan president Akasaka says that Japan has lost half of its foreign correspondents in the last decade. They've moved on to other countries where things seem to be happening more. What results is a perception gap between what is happening here and what the world thinks is happening here. To the world, Japan seems less important, although Republican presidential candidate Donald Trump has managed to make it more important again by lumping China and Japan together in his stump speeches: "We are gonna bring back jobs from China. We are gonna bring back jobs from Japan." Trump has said that Prime Minister Shinzo Abe is "really smart" and said about U.S. Ambassador to Japan Caroline Kennedy: "She'll do anything they (Japan) want. Anything."

Whenever I have to go anywhere in Tokyo for the first time, I check Google Maps and look for the Access button. With one click, it tells me how far by train, taxi, or foot I am to the location. The key message that Japan needs to convey to rest of the world is that Japan as a country is accessible and foreign-friendly. Japan is local and more global than it lets on. You can find a burger or pizza here. It is not too inscrutable for amateurs. Too much of Japan's promotion to the world caters to Japan specialists and foreign elites, like luxury travelers. The current Japan National Tourism Office (JNTO) catchphrase, "Japan, Endless Discovery," replaced "Yokoso! Japan," the Japanese word for welcome that is not understood by most non-natives.

The number of international visitors to Japan was 6.79 million in 2009. In 2015 that number increased to 19.7 million,[114] but Hong Kong, China, South Korea, Malaysia, and Thailand still boost higher numbers. In 2014 Japan ranked 22nd globally for annual total visitors, seventh in Asia with travelers totaling 13.4 million. That compares with the 83.7 million who traveled to France, 74.8 million who traveled to the United States and the 65 million who traveled to China, the top three nations on the list in 2014. Just 400,000 international visitors came to Japan in 1964, the year of Tokyo's first Olympics.

Global people do not automatically think of Japan as a top tourist destination—maybe a dream, but not a reality. The main image hurdles are language and cost barriers. To its credit, JNTO added an "Affordable Japan" section to its website (jnto.go.jp). The yen has weakened, which explains the big uptick in visitors. Japan is now more affordable, but the perception of a wealth gap between it and other countries will persist among people who reside outside of the Asian region. The language barrier is a real problem. At 1.5 billion English language learners, English is the most dominant language studied in the world as a second language.[115] Mandarin Chinese has more native speakers, but there is no language that matches the number of growing English communicators. We've got to dispel the reputation that English has as a cultural imperialist language in Japan. Learning English doesn't make you less Japanese. Learning English makes you more universal. It's inexcusable that English is not taught in Japan until junior high. Japan's East Asian neighbors (and regional competitors) are studying English as elementary school children, if not sooner. Even in Tokyo, foreign visitors have told me how surprised they are by the lack of English communication at international hotels. A European group of first-time visitors at a 2014 conference in Keio University told me that they thoroughly enjoyed Japan but were not likely to return because there were many other Asian countries where they could communicate better.

Here in Japan there is still an in-group/out-group approach to global communication and understanding, as there is in Asia. Japan sees itself as somewhat apart from Asia, and this is a mistake. It needs to be a global and Asian leader. "Japan's original sin lies in its attempts to separate itself from Asia," as R. Taggart Murphy says in *Japan and the Shackles of the Past*.

I'm constantly asked, "What can Japan (including the Japanese government, general public and businesses) do more to promote Japanese brand to outside the country towards 2020?" Here are some suggestions:

· Promote Japan as a global destination, not just unique Japan
· Emphasize safety/security, two major concerns of international visitors
· Embrace those who are Japanophiles and not necessarily Japanophones

Every globally-engaged Japanese citizen needs to recognize himself or herself as integral to Japan's foreign relations. My NHK friend, Hatsuhisa Takashima, says, "The greatest weakness of Japan lies in its citizens who do not realize that they are directly linked to global efforts to disseminate information about Japan."[116] I couldn't agree more.

Kiyotaka Akasaka, president of the Foreign Press Center of Japan (Japan's public diplomacy arm of the government), says that if there are any active domestic discussions in Japan, people overseas are unaware of them, thus leading the world to assume that Japan does not have a global voice. He stresses the importance of Japan having media tools that are influential worldwide, together with nurturing talented individuals with a global perspective.

Japan can always do more. This is not my message. The Japanese experts I talk to tell me this. They know already that Japan does not have strengths in global strategic communication. That's a reality. Let's do something about this. One of the ways to elevate Japan in the world is to identify its core strengths. One of those I easily recognize as an International Relations professor is Japan's strength in ODA (official development assistance). Japan needs to share a lot more stories about its work with international organizations, both officially from the PMO and Cabinet Office of Japan, but also unofficially at the grassroots. There are many globally active Japanese, not all are business entrepreneurs. We need to strengthen their ability to market what they do. I'd also like to emphasize stories that aren't just about new security bills and economics. Abenomics and changes to Japan's security apparatus (US-Japan Security Alliance) are big global media stories, but they can drown out stories about Japan's role in the UN and its multinational diplomacy efforts. I worry that Japan's national brand may be diluted if it decreases its contributions in the areas of environmental preservation, arms reduction, and human rights in favor of military and national or economic security concerns.

There seems to be an impression that Japan's promoters and Japan's media think us foreign folk all like the same things: cuisine, popular or traditional culture. Some of us just like the novelty of a place that allows us to be minorities with some privilege status because we aren't Japanese. We like the "fish out of water" extreme of visiting or living here. It is not one specific thing. There are often questions about "How do you like Japan?" "Do you like Japanese food?" Some of these questions are just emblematic of Japanese reserve and politeness. I like to talk about Japan's cultural contradictions, the darker aspects of Japan in certain industries, advertising images, the press system, the political establishment, but I know that my intellectual and probing interests do not always mesh well with polite company that hovers more around cultural artifacts.

JAPAN'S ORIGINAL PUBLIC DIPLOMATS: TOKUGAWA AND FUKUZAWA

This book is being released just over five years after the Great East Japan earthquake, tsunami, and nuclear meltdown we know as 3/11. Prime Minister Naoto Kan of the Democratic Party of Japan called it the worst disaster Japan had faced since World War II. In marked contrast to 3/11 as an evergreen symbol of devastation and mourning, 3/11 will also signify a rebirth and renewal of my professional and personal life. I received congratulatory news during the week of March 11, 2011. A notification letter arrived from the Japan-U.S. Educational Commission in Tokyo that I had earned a Fulbright scholarship to return to Japan to teach American foreign policy and American culture at the prestigious Jesuit Catholic institution of higher education, Sophia University. Given the proximity to Japan's worst natural disaster, you can imagine my ambivalent feelings about my exchange opportunity. I was full of joy for this second Fulbright award (my first was as a student to the Federal Republic of Germany), but very worried about the consequences for this country going forward. Would this post-3/11 era be a New Normal[117] for Japan as it had been, albeit briefly, for my home country after 9/11? Anger soon followed personal joy as I learned about the human failings (institutional lying) by Tepco in reporting the facts about how awful the fallout actually was at the Fukushima Daiichi nuclear power plant. And how preventable. Niigata Prefecture Governor Hirohiko Izumida said more than two and a half years later: "There are three things required of a company that runs nuclear power plants: don't lie, keep your promises and fulfill your social responsibility."[118] While the people in charge of companies were not being held accountable, it was the Japanese citizenry and workers at the nuclear power plant that kept their promises.

Like my fellow global citizens, I was awestruck at the heroism of what the international press called the "Fukushima 50," those plant workers who stayed behind at much personal peril to health and safety to prevent a national disaster from growing into an international calamity. We opened up our hearts and pocketbooks to Japan in response to the model display of dignity and a national psyche of calm and perseverance in the face of so much anxiety and unknown. That March of 2011, I was Professor of Communications at California State University, Fullerton. Sitting as I was in sunny Southern California watching the news video feeds out of Japan, I didn't think that my fellow compatriots would have acted quite so orderly in response to disaster. I was thankful to see so many public figures and governments around the world respond with international humanitarian assistance, which the government of Japan readily accepted this time, unlike its refusal to accept outside help after the Great Hanshin Earthquake (Kobe earthquake) of 1995. Even Lady Gaga ("Lady Gaga-san") took charge with a Twitter diplomacy effort to encourage her "little monsters" to #PrayForJapan and donate over $3 million to relief efforts. Just four months after 3/11, she visited Japan to show the world that the country was still very much intact and open for visitors. "I can't say enough to people all over the world that the majority of Japan right now, Japan in general, is very safe. It's fine to come here. It's beautiful."[119]

Just over a year after March 11, I was teaching a few minutes from the Imperial Palace in the city formerly known as Edo, with signs marking my district neighborhood Rokubancho as the living quarters for the *hatamoto*, the samurai who directly served the Tokugawa shogun. I was far removed from feudal Japan, but what I did conclude early on was that today's Japan—its awkward embrace with the world—is a direct descendant behavior of two looming figures in Japanese history. The first represents the closing off and the second represents the opening up. Both have lessons for embracing global learning.

Tokugawa Ieyasu was the founding shogun responsible for establishing a national seclusion policy (*sakoku*) in the 1630s, effectively cutting off Japan from the world, with a few exceptions for Chinese and Dutch traders in the port of Nagasaki, 1,229 kilometers from Edo. Why this isolation policy happened had a lot to do with a xenophobic response to Christian missionaries from Portugal and

Spain. Christianity was an imported religion thought to be subversive to Japanese society. A case could be made for that since Christian Catholicism represented an alternative form of devotion to a higher order than loyalty to an earthbound military establishment.

The isolation worked wonders. The people developed a particularly Japanese way of doing things, making it to their own specifications. This should sound as familiar to the postwar period of modern Japan in the 20th century as it did to the 17th century artisans, merchants, and peasant classes who were subordinates to the professional warrior class known as samurai. This cultural DNA of isolation and seclusion is the background music ambiance to any conversation about Japan's going global today.

I don't view this inward-looking heritage as quite a negative precursor to all of Japan's challenges today. It is more like a mixed blessing. Under a very strict military protectorate with a strong bureaucratic structure, Japan was able to raise its literacy to a world-leading 30 percent, which, in turn, led to commercial publishing and the founding of private schools. During the early Tokugawa era, the population doubled from approximately 15 million in 1600 to 30 million by 1700. The peasants in the rural areas of Japan represented 90 percent of the population. Merchants and artisans who lived in the cities were not held in as high regard as the peasants and farmers who directly provided subsistence to the people. The Neo-Confucianism philosophy emphasized developing human relations along the lines of the hegemonic moral authority of the samurai class:

A military government ruling as feudal autocrats, bakufu policy tended to be conservative, authoritarian, concerned mainly with maintaining social order. Neo-Confucianism focuses on human relationships of loyalty, cooperation, and obedience to superiors, and this was easily adapted to the hierarchical feudalism of Tokugawa Japan, especially in the Japanese interpretation of the Chinese Confucian virtue of "conscientious sincerity" as "unwavering loyalty to the state.[120]

The Tokugawa shogunate (*bakufu*) is impressive for securing two centuries of a peaceful Japan until black ships (the black was the smoke emitting from the coal-burning steam) with a Commodore of the U.S. Navy showed up in Tokyo Bay with a new form of international persuasion. In a letter to the Emperor of Japan, President Millard Fillmore wrote: "I have directed Commodore Perry to assure your imperial majesty that I entertain the kindest feelings toward your majesty's person and government, and that I have no other object in sending him to Japan but to propose to your imperial majesty that the United States and Japan should live in friendship and have commercial intercourse with each other."[121] Such intercourse was not of the one-night stand variety but what could be called a long period of engagement with a major break-up during World War II.

Over time the US-Japan engagement has naturally led to a stronger identification with the West than with the East. No longer are outside persons (*Gaijin*) considered full-fledged barbarians or isolated on the fan-shaped Dejima (Exit Island) in Nagasaki Bay. During the Meiji Restoration, Japanese began going abroad to learn Western ways and to integrate new ways of thinking into Japan's societal development from economy to education.

Enter a second leading figure in Japan's development. He's not the only one, but the one who continues to inspire. For many reasons I call him the Benjamin Franklin of Japan. We are most familiar with his face which appears on the ¥10,000 currency note. I'm very moved by the philosophy of Fukuzawa Yukichi, and what he had to say about Japan's efforts at public speaking and public presentation. I may not have much sophisticated grasp or embrace of the Japanese language, but over time I've developed a sense of what matters most to Japanese people. One of those things is a simple and subtle approach to beauty and communication. It's actually a very sophisticated model of communicating because we overlook the simple and beautiful in our everyday, techno-driven engagements. We miss out on the most obvious, and Japanese sensibility, as explained by Fukuzawa, encourages us that acts of revolution begin with independent thought and mutual understanding. He encouraged us all to be scholars of life's undertakings, and that is a most simple recommendation. In his most famous book, he was writing at a time when Japan was embracing the world, embracing the West, really looking out to the West as a learning model, not as a superior model to duplicate, but rather as a respected teacher to help Japan advance itself. And he understood the spiritual side of who we are together on this planet:

> Japan and the nations of the West are peoples who live between the same heaven and earth, feel the warmth of the same sun, look up at the same moon, share the same oceans and air, and possess the same human feelings. Therefore, nations that have should share with those that have not. We should mutually teach and learn from each other, without shame or pride. We should promote each other's interests and pray for each other's happiness. We should associate with one another following the laws of Heaven and humanity.[122]

Now why do I share this quote in a book about Japan's information war with the world? I share it because a scholar, journalist, philosopher and leader from 100 years ago matters as much now as he did then. He can provide answers. I don't have the answers. I'm an observer and can share some "needs improvement" recommendations, but I remain a guest in Japan, a very privileged guest, but a guest. I observe the culture. I observe the ways that Japanese communicate externally and internally, especially the way that the government of Japan communicates with the world. That's my specialty. Why I care so much about Fukuzawa is that he's Japan's greatest teacher. He's been one of my great teachers. It was during my Abe fellowship at Keio University that I discovered Fukuzawa's leadership in global education. I'm not sure that I would have ever discovered him on my own of course. Whenever I have a ¥10,000 note in my hand I'm reminded of him. I like having ¥10,000 notes in my hands, but more than that, I like what he represents because he is one of the greatest currencies for improving Japan's global communication. The next time you look at a ¥10,000 note, think of it in the context of public relations and not just commerce.

Here's why else I like Professor Fukuzawa. In his book, *An Encouragement of Learning*, he talks about showing deference to government officials, not because of the status that these officials have as office holders, but rather because of the duties that these officials have to act on behalf of the Japanese people in policy and laws that impact everyone. It's a very healthy philosophy to have. He encouraged his students at Keio to engage in public debates. The Enzetsukan (Speakers' Hall) is the building on the Keio Mita campus where these debates took place. Built in 1875, it serves as a bit of a relic to Japan's early modern appreciation for the role of a university as a place to exchange ideas in a public venue.

Fukuzawa is credited with translating the English word "speech" into the Japanese word *enzetsu*. His style of communication is described as "colloquial and comprehensible even for the less educated. In the face of the general skeptical opinion that the Japanese language did not lend itself to oratory, he started public speaking and conducted open debates."[123]

There is no more important text to better understand how these new ideas were implemented than Yukichi Fukuzawa's *An Encouragement of Learning* (*Gakumon no Susume*), a collection of 17 pamphlets published during the early Meiji Period (1872-1876). I do not profess to know much about Fukuzawa before I started using Japanese currency. The same might be said of a foreign scholar to the U.S. who knows little about Benjamin Franklin before exchanging currency. Unlike the Fukuzawa yen note however, the Franklin $100 bill has entered the vernacular through popular music like P. Diddy's 1997 song, "It's All About the Benjamins," and the 2002 action comedy film, *All About the Benjamins*, co-written and starring rapper Ice Cube. (I once made a mistake in a presentation at Waseda University where I tried to be a bit hip and explain how policy follows money. I said, "It's all about the Benjamins," and my translator responded, "I'm sorry, Benjamins?") I should remember not to use so much street slang in my public presentations, but alas, that's part of American English to use a lot of catchphrases and cliches.

Fukuzawa is as deserving of a song and movie title as Benjamin Franklin. He's performed the role of international statesman, educator, and public figure. His instructions to his people in how to educate oneself are comparable to Benjamin Franklin, who, like Fukuzawa, founder of Keio University, established a leading private university, University of Pennsylvania. Unlike Franklin, Fukuzawa stayed out of politics, but he explained that the politician was never above the law and that any respect that a politician had was a result of his involvement with the making of laws, not because of his having political status. This was a democratic milestone to a Tokugawa military government. As such, both Tokugawa and Fukuzawa deserve their place in Japan's public diplomacy history as bookend visionaries of what Japan has become.

NICE NANCY IN NICE JAPAN

I have a thing about nice. Well, actually I'm fixated on nice. Sometimes nice, which denotes pleasure, goodness, or coolness (Nice Car!) can have diametrically opposed meanings. (Just look up "nice" at Aaron Peckham's Urban Dictionary.) If a friend is trying to set you up with someone and says he or she is "nice," that can be the kiss of death in dating lingo. It could mean that nice actually means "boring" or nice actually means "not so attractive, but pleasant-enough looking." He's nice or she's nice can translate into make that a coffee instead of a dinner, definitely not a potential overnight guest prospect. Presidential candidate Barack Obama once called Hillary Clinton "likeable enough" and he definitely wasn't being nice in the traditional sense.

My growing up involved a lot of references to "nice Nancy" or "Nancy is nice." As an adult I'm known to be professionally nice (pleasant, easygoing, helpful), which I'm happy to own, but there is also a "Nice Nancy Syndrome" that I feel lurking beneath the surface. Being nice can be exhausting. Being nice as a writer and scholar means that I hear from people around the world who know that I'm nice enough to consider reading their book manuscript, sitting on their dissertation review committee or reading those college entrance examinations. I want to tell them that Nice Nancy is just me, not Nice Nancy, Inc. Also, does being nice have an off button? Can I be not so nice?

Let's move this analogy to an entire country. Japan is known around the world for its niceness. The people are nice. The people are nicely dressed. The conveniences are nice. The food is really, really nice. The trains run nicely on time. The small dogs, treated like babies, seem nice, if a bit lethargic. Cool Japan isn't really the nice face of Japan but a marketing scheme.

The true face of Japan is "Nice Japan."

So when someone somewhere says, "I'd like to go somewhere nice" in reference to an overseas visit, then Japan is often at the top of that list. A whole country of nice is much better than a country known for extreme poverty, civil wars, loud and angry outbursts, and terrorism. You get the picture.

Andrew Tuck, editor at *Monocle* magazine says about Japan, "Having good manners shouldn't be difficult but a country as well behaved as Japan has turned being nice into an art." As he points out, we have global indices for friendliness and happiness, but "niceness is harder to measure and a bit deeper and more valuable than just friendliness. And if I was in charge of marketing for Japan, I'd be bottling it and selling it. Being nice is nice."[124]

What a wonderful endorsement of Japan. What can possibly go wrong? Remember what I said about the Nice Nancy Syndrome. The same thing can happen to Japan. Niceness in nation branding can be fatiguing and this is a country known for its hard-working population, death by overwork and putting in such long work days that the government had to step in to insist that Japanese take at least half of their mandatory paid vacations (minimally two weeks), which too many workers avoid altogether.

Japan's reputation for nice will be put to the test with the Tokyo 2020 Summer Olympic Games. When Tokyo won the summer Olympics host bid in September 2013, it defeated competitors Istanbul and Madrid by reputation as the "safe hands" alternative. Prime Minister Abe assured people everywhere that any radiation worries about the Fukushima-Daichi plant were "under control" and he guaranteed a safe and successful Olympics. [125] Three-quarters of Japanese surveyed said that they didn't believe the prime minister's pledge that the situation at Fukushima-Daiichi was under control.[126] With so much questioning of political credibility at home, how can Japan expect the world to react but with the same skepticism?

In 2015 nice Japan was challenged by the Abe's administration push to change a global reputation for nicely pacifist Japan constitutionally mandated for self-defense forces. What we have seen created overnight (September 19, 2015) is an outward-looking and assertive nation with a modern military trained to intervene if "a foreign country in a close relationship with Japan" comes under attack.[127] Being consistently nice, we know now, takes some effort to maintain.

Perhaps the true test for nice Japan will come not so much from the Prime Minister's Office or the Diet, but at the frontline among those serving the droves of visitors who will descend on the nation, as they are now doing with the falling yen. My friendly 7-Eleven lady who always has a smile comes to mind or the nice guy at Lawson who carefully adds the four creams, stirs to mix, and packages my iced espresso. As one British resident in Japan put it, "Retail staff in the shops and conbinis and rail staff are the folk who will be at the front line in dealing with hordes of visitors in 2020. They are amongst Japan's most hard-working, polite and welcoming of citizens. Whilst everyone else is at work in their offices, they will be knee deep in barbarians from across the seas. Surely they all deserve a really good bonus as Japan's ambassadors of first contact during the Games." [128] Notwithstanding the barbarians from across the seas image, the British resident makes an excellent point: Japan's everyday people are Japan's brand in the world. It would behoove the Japanese government to be more inclusive in the people's perspective in shaping the direction and management of Japan's nation brand long before 2020 arrives.

JAPAN AND CHINA

GUESS WHO'S NOT COMING TO DINNER?

Ralph K. White, a psychologist who studied the political relationship between the United States and the Soviet Union once said, "When one country is coming up from behind and is about equal to another country, that is where tension is highest, like two racehorses, side-by-side, that are straining every nerve to get ahead of the other."

White is the author of *Nobody Wanted War* and *Fearful Warriors*. Like me, Dr. White worked at the United States Information Agency, and he is one of the most influential scholars in explaining what leads nations to war.

The racehorses of today are the United States, China and Japan. The U.S., despite a resilient economic downturn, remains the world's fastest racehorse. It's those other two racehorses, China and Japan, that are straining their nerves to get ahead in socioeconomic and national security influence.

We often forget that nation-states are comprised first and foremost of people. It is people—their fears, motivations, attitudes, and beliefs—that drive international relations. One of the most contentious relationships these days is a new Cold War ideological showdown between the world's second and third largest economies. Historically speaking, the two countries hate each other. And the enmity is growing. Recent Pew research polls show that neither country can get out of the single digits in favoring the other. There is no friendship ring of "hands across Northeast Asia." It's one big "dislike" button, despite droves of Chinese tourists coming to Japan for shopping and the highest percentage of foreign students (94,000+), over half of all foreign students (184,000) coming to Japan's universities for study in 2015.[129]

Japan, the post-World War II economic miracle the size of Montana, was once second to the world's largest economy, the United States. But in 2011, Japan lost its "place" showing to China. That shift from second to third, combined with a hard fall from the economic halcyon days when it was "the Japan that can say no," leads Japan, and its present nation brand leader, Shinzo Abe, to project an image of power and strength that is most visible in its standing up to China. In Abe's effort to reignite respect and reverence for Japan's economy and national security state, he has generated more fear and insecurity, and not just from China, but from the world.

Abe's December 26, 2013 controversial visit to Yasukuni Shrine stands as an example not of Japan's strength but of what Ralph K. White would call an unhealthy, even somewhat paranoid fear of a rising China, a fear similar to that which existed for over forty years between the US and USSR. China and Japan's words and actions promote exaggerated fears based on a diabolical enemy image. When two countries mirror each other this way, there is no opportunity for any everlasting peace, just some silent hope that things won't get worse such as an incident or accident that would lead to war.

If the world saw Abe's Yasukuni visit as good for international relations, then we'd all be quoting from Abe's pledge for everlasting peace, which he made the same day he dressed in his best for his Yasukuni visit. But no one can remember that speech when the picture of Abe at the war dead shrine is what dominated headlines. The world saw the prime minister engaged in a propaganda battle between China and Japan. In such a role, he is viewed as an instigator, not a mediator, an inciter, not a bridge builder.

Abe's pledge for everlasting peace was certainly hopeful: "Japan must never wage a war again. "Japan must be a country which joins hands with friends in Asia and friends around the world to realize peace of the entire world." But words soon fall empty when actions drive fears that reinforce antipathy and lack of respect between neighbors.

When two people hate each other, it's easy to imagine a war of words or fights breaking out. Nations are no different.

As one who has lived and taught in both Beijing and Tokyo—I don't believe that the enmity between these two proud global capitals will end. There is a domestic pay-off to pointing the accusatory finger at the other. Real tensions exist and persist, despite the strong trade ties and foreign investment. Where there is a possibility for positive change is at the grassroots level where you can work side-by-side with people and see the effect you are making. In 2007 the dean of Tsinghua University's School of Journalism and Communication asked me to remain in China to help the country improve its media relations with the foreign press during the Beijing Olympics. While stateside circumstances precluded me from staying beyond my sabbatical semester, my time there in sharing my media relations expertise with state officials and my discussions about politics and media with Tsinghua students converted me into a Sinophile. I'm also a Japanophile who now lives part-time in Tokyo.

I love my two Asian host countries for what makes them most appealing—the people. It's easy to take issue with governments, their respective human rights records, or the political rhetoric of their leadership. But the lasting positive impression resides with the people—the friends I have in Beijing and Tokyo. It pains my heart that there aren't more visible efforts to build bridges of friendship and mutual respect between Japan and China.

We might begin with an open heart and an empty stomach.

It was in Beijing where a Tsinghua colleague told me that my enthusiasm for Chinese culture and cuisine made me a favorite among the faculty. He compared my positive nature to that of another American visiting professor who was quick to complain about slow Internet speed on campus or bureaucratic red tape. I had the same challenges as my complaining American colleague, but I viewed my visiting professorship as equivalent to being a guest for dinner in someone's home. You are there to show graciousness and appreciation for all that your host has to offer you.

Imagine if the citizens of China and Japan could step outside the mutual enemy images that drive their relations to the level of a dinner companion in one's home. Imagine if the people of these two super economic powers could make an ongoing public effort to learn and listen more about each other's hopes and dreams for Asia's future.

So far, the voices of the citizens of Japan and China are relatively silent while the dueling rhetoric of ambassadors and heads of state dominate. It's like turning on one channel, Hate TV, designed to incite more fear and anger. Isn't it time for a new channel?

WINNING AND LOSING HEARTS AND MINDS

Speech presented to the Platform for International Policy Dialogue (PIPD), Ministry of Finance, Tokyo, Japan, June 10, 2015.

In everything I do and know about Japan's public diplomacy, let me always thank the Japanese taxpayers. My understanding of Japan comes almost exclusively from the generosity of the Japanese government. With the exception of about two weeks of sponsored talks paid for by the U.S. State Department and Embassy of the US in Tokyo, all of my time in country has been the result of the Japanese government's invitation to come and discover Japan. This includes the Japan-US Educational Commission (Fulbright Japan), the Japan Foundation (Abe Fellowship), and the Prime Minister's Office (International Youth Village, Japan-American Leadership Exchange Committee). What I'm about to say is the result of that government-sponsored study.

My writings and speeches about Japan's brand image in the world are like the proverbial canary in a coalmine. While canaries warned of danger, I can also function like the glass globe buoys of Otaru that alerted fishermen about where to catch herring. So I wish to point out yellow tape warnings as well as green light positive paths for a more effective public diplomacy.

Today it is Japan that is the true canary. Japan's problems, be it low fertility, an aging population, natural disasters, low resources, weakened economy, abandoned towns and villages, single moms in poverty, are not just Japan's problems to solve. Many of these problems loom for other advanced industrialized market democracies. This is why Japan's better understanding of itself, in an unvarnished "warts and all" manner, is exceedingly important, not just for Japan, but also for its place in the world. And that process will require more involvement of the Japanese people from across generation, wealth, occupation and gender. In order for Japan to win more global sympathy, it will have to increase the depth and breadth of its storytelling. I know it can do this because I first learned about

Japan through watching old Japanese films by Ozu and Kurasawa, specifically *Tokyo Story* and *Ikiru*, among others, that helped me to see family and society in a different light.

In order for Japan to better tell its story to the world, I offer a few modest suggestions:

1. It's time to graduate beyond personality and partisanship in public diplomacy. Branding Japan requires a nation branding process that exceeds the current occupants of The Diet and the Prime Minister's Office. Whenever countries place too much attention on their political leaders, the nation falls when the personal brand of that politician falls. My best example is Barack Obama, whose favorability numbers in June 2015, according to a CNN poll, were below that of his predecessor, George W. Bush (45% to 52%).[130] At the time Bush left office in January 2009, just one third of voters approved of him. Ups and downs in political credibility and likeability happen to all politicians and it is happening here. Political dynasties are about preserving power and are inefficient as well as insufficient carriers of a nation's global projection.

2. Japan's public diplomacy is heavy on culture promotion but culture promotion alone won't win more adherents to Japan's place in the world. If I eat sushi do I support Japan's policies? No, I just eat sushi, and sushi has transcended Japan. Over thirty years ago during Japan's go-go economy years, the *New York Times'* Jack Rosenthal, a Pulitzer Prize winning editorial writer, wrote a column about the opening of a sushi restaurant inside the Harvard Club.[131] He said, "The presence of a sushi bar at the Harvard Club suggests something more than tolerating Japanese manufactures; it suggests a genuine curiosity and welcome for aspects of Japanese culture. In a small way, it signals a new cultural convergence." An article in the men's magazine *Esquire* called "Wake Up Little Sushi" later became a TV series.

Sushi is Japan's origin but is so widely franchised today in all sorts of ventures (e.g. sold at baseball stadiums), that it has diluted its meaning as the official food emblem of Japan. (I vote soba as the next sushi, because the world doesn't know soba as well and needs to know that the Japanese eat more than sushi.) There may be a loose association between sushi and Japan like there is with Hello Kitty (i.e., an Islamist fighter using a Hello Kitty notebook) but once a product goes global, no nation gets to control its embedded messages. Otherwise we could presume that a militant leader, with his Hello Kitty notebook, has some affection for Japan.

Japanese cuisine *(Washoku)* is popular among a certain segment of the global population and Japan has a well-deserved high rating in its overall quality, safety, presentation and taste. Japanese cuisine is now listed as a UNESCO Intangible Cultural Heritage and sushi is enjoyed the world over, but Japan needs to be more strategic about relating culture to reputation gains. *Jiro Dreams of Sushi* (2011) was a hit not just because of the Japanese name Jiro and Sushi in the title but mostly because it tells an excellent and entertaining good story. Many of our stories come from our dreams, daydreaming and night dreaming, and Japan is no different.

Japan is currently not recognized enough as a nation of storytellers, but there is no reason it cannot be so if you make storytelling the main feature of how you want to better communicate with the world. There may be a partial explanation here. In many societies, good storytelling is associated with oral communication passed down from generation to generation. We sometimes call it spinning a good yarn, the kind of good conversation you might have while knitting. Japanese studies scholars point out that public speaking and speaking well or skillfully hold more negative than positive connotations. There are proverbs (smart in words, weak in deeds; an empty drum thunders loudly; a mewing cat will not catch a mouse). In contrast, a European or American tends to place a higher value on good public speaking and making a powerful argument in public. Kanayama (1988) said, "The Japanese are suspicious about skillful public speakers." It's very common for me to hear from Japanese I've interviewed that "We aren't the best promoters," or "We aren't very good at public relations."

3. It's time to get beyond Cool Japan to telling/sharing Japan's stories, commercial or not, with the world. Cool Japan's stated purpose is to "win the sympathy of other countries," making it part of Japan's official public diplomacy campaign. All public diplomacy

is based in an environment of political economy and national security but there is no evidence that a strong correlation exists between buying Japanese comic books and sympathizing with Japanese policies. The Cool Japan Promotion Council report released in August 2014 attributes the popularity of Zen in the United States to Steve Jobs' import of his study of Japanese Zen Buddhism. "The creation of many innovative products by Steve Jobs, who studied Japanese Zen Buddhism, has helped to popularize Zen in many places in the United States." Zen Buddhism is not a popular practice, but Zen, the word, is used everywhere. Very few Americans, much less the world, will associate Apple products with Japanese Zen Buddhism, however much we want to take the leap between the two. Apple is known for its simple and understated designs with functionality, which is part of Japanese design sensibility (economy of means, exquisite detailing), but it's not an automatic Japan-to-Apple correlation in the minds of the world.

I read *Zen and the Art of Motorcycle Maintenance* in high school. It was required reading before entering the university. If you travel the pages of the world's largest online bookseller, Amazon.com, you will see hundreds of books that use Zen in the title. They range from cooking (*The Zen of Frosting*) to drinking (*Zen and Tonic*) to golf (*Zen and the Art of Making Par*), to archery (*Zen in the Art of Archery*). Hence, Zen, like Sushi, is everyone's vocabulary today. Do we think of Germany when we hear the word kindergarten?

4. Japan's public diplomacy must be targeted for people, if not more so, than for governments. The state-centric model of international promotion is outmoded. We need a citizen-oriented model that includes new models of representation such as citizens' panels. In the U.S. one can be summoned to serve on a jury. Why not have Japanese citizens summoned to serve in the national public interests of their country, free of government restriction? Why is so much of Japan's official representation in the world highlighted by political strife and discord, be it WWII legacy disputes or textbook revisions? There are exceptions and of late I've been introduced to a very positive development in Japan's public diplomacy—Japan House. Modeled in part on the Scandinavian House in New York

City, this public-private partnership will create Japan House ventures in three major cities of power and influence in the world: Los Angeles, London, and Sao Paulo. These houses are still at the concept level but they are meant to be centers of dialogue, exhibit, conversation, and yes, some commercial engagement, but mostly places where people of all persuasions, ethnicities and nationalities can develop their minds. What I especially like is that the Japan House ventures will be led by a local secretariat in each respective city. The locals are the eyes and ears of what works, what appeals, and those participating are community leaders but not necessarily Japan experts.

5. Let me share some surprising statistics about today's information and communication technologies. Most everyone (75%) now has access to mobile phone technology, which allows for short message service (SMS) and Interactive Voice Response (IVR). By 2020, that number should rise to 90% of all persons on the planet age six and older who will have mobile phone access. In contrast, only 40% of the world has Internet access, and in certain continents, notably Africa, that figure is much higher. In Africa, almost 20 per cent of the population is now online, up from 10 per cent in 2010. In the Asia-Pacific region, one third is now online. Japan's nation brand reflects a high tech, soft touch set of principles. It should be using its technology to increase global connectivity and to promote global transparency. New media, including mobile and social media, can help to demystify Japanese society and encourage more global interest and participation. Japanese public diplomacy staff leadership is on a shoestring budget but for a relatively low cost could seek out better interactions with civil society and the media.

6. In the spirit of greater transparency and accountability in serving global society, Japan needs to share more information with the world. There is a mystery and secrecy surrounding some of what Japan is and does. There is an expression, "information abhors a vacuum." When there is a void, people fill in that space with their own preconceived notions and stereotypes. It's important that Japan define itself to the world on its own terms and not play catch up or constantly play defense attempting to explain things after the fact. Be

proactive. There is also a time when it's best not to say anything. In Japan especially, silence is golden. It is thought that dynamic public speakers are less trustworthy because they are persuasive in a flashier sense. The Japanese sensibility is to value the less talented presenter who humbles oneself before the audience.

I'd like to encourage Japan to build more accessible databases of statistical and other information on its society and do this in a multilanguage platform. I came across a most fascinating collection of data on Japanese self-images compiled by the Institute of Statistical Mathematics. The data set covers seven decades (1958-2008) and shows that Japanese self-images are quite consistent across time. In answer to the question about which words represent the characteristics of the Japanese, the top choices were diligent (55-72%), courteous, kind, and persevering (46-60%). Idealistic ranged from 20-32% (highest in 1958); Rational (8-22%); Liberal (9-17%); Easygoing (11-19%); and Cheerful (8-23%). The lowest choice was Creative (7-11%). The Cool Japan Promotion Council report mentions the results of an Adobe Systems, Inc. survey in 2012 that polled 1,000 people in five countries: UK, France, Germany, Japan, and the U.S. Among the global respondents, Japan was chosen the most creative country and Tokyo the most creative city. The Japanese respondents chose the U.S. as the most creative country and NYC as the most creative city. A majority of American respondents identified themselves as creative (52%).

7. Japan's public diplomacy (JPD) is more than what Joseph Nye says or what you think he said—it's beyond time for Japan to develop its own scholars/practitioners. JPD needs ties to the academy with curriculum development in PD, PR, Global Media Studies, Public Opinion and Media Relations Management. It's not soft power versus hard power. It's all about power and influence. PD is more than nation branding—it's regional collaboration and place branding.

8. Finally, strengthen the narrative. It's not clear what Japan's story is to the world. What are Japanese values that need more promotion? A Cool Japan report states that it's all about building sympathy in the world. Winning hearts and minds? That's too

unclear. You need a strategic plan. Do more research ahead of public information campaigns. Tap into the critics as well as Japan champion networks. Hire more international faculty to carry the message of Japan to the world. Let's pull up our sleeves now. There is work to be done.

U.S. PUBLIC DIPLOMACY LESSONS FOR JAPAN

BUSH TO OBAMA

Based on a speech for an international conference, "America in Global Asia," Sophia University, Tokyo, Japan, March 9, 2013

The term public diplomacy (PD) is an America Cold War creation that has gone global. It is credited to Dean Edmund Gullion of the Fletcher School of Law and Diplomacy, Tufts University, at the founding of the Edward R. Murrow Center for Public Diplomacy in 1965.[132] PD is perpetually associated with three arenas of scholarly inquiry: public opinion formulation, foreign policy, and communication. As such, a Murrow Center brochure defined public diplomacy as "the cause and effect of public attitudes and opinions which influence the formulation and execution of foreign policy. It encompasses dimensions of international relations beyond traditional diplomacy; the cultivation by governments of public opinion in other countries; the interaction of private groups and interests in one country with those of another; the reporting of foreign affairs and its impact on policy; communication between those whose job is communication, as between diplomats and foreign correspondents; and the processes of intercultural communications. Central to public diplomacy is the transnational flow of information and ideas."[133]

In today's fast-paced global communications environment where one might just have seconds to explain what public diplomacy is to a fellow elevator passenger, I would suggest the following: An international actor's attempt to advance the ends of policy by engaging with foreign publics.

Public diplomacy has everything to do with international persuasion and social influence. Properly understood and applied, it is a long-term essential of influence strategy and national security. It is a function and concern of all nations, from multinational organizations such as the European Union and United Nations to nation branding institutions like the Japan Foundation and the

British Council. Traditional public diplomacy actors include public affairs and public information officers of the government, government broadcasters, and cultural mediators like sponsored exchange students and international aid field workers.[134] Elements of public diplomacy include the following: active listening, advocacy for one's side, cultural diplomacy, international exchange, international broadcasting, and psychological warfare.[135]

Today's new public diplomacy expands the breadth and depth of influence agents, who now include public figures and institutions that may at times challenge prevailing elite assumptions in international relations and foreign policies of government (e.g., international terrorists, sports stars, celebrities, NGOs.) Take, for example, the public diplomacy engagement by Dennis "The Worm" Rodman, the former NBA star who traveled with the Harlem Globe Trotters to the People's Republic of North Korea. Rodman declared Kim Jong Un a "friend for life" after the two enjoyed a dinner and basketball game. Early in his arrival, Rodman had tweeted, "Maybe I'll run into the Gangnam Style dude while I'm here" in reference to South Korean capital Seoul, and not Pyongyang, North Korea, which got a quick response from South Korean rapper Psy, "I'm from #South, man!!!"

Rodman's short-term sports diplomacy visit to North Korea illustrates how any international person of influence, including a retired professional basketball star with a less than credible public reputation in his country of origin, can engage foreign publics on policy. Rodman may have made communication mistakes during his PRNK visit, but like any other celebrity from sports or entertainment, his mere presence in a foreign country, especially one as closed off to free society as North Korea, is enough for a public diplomacy spectacle to occur. This almost comical "bromance" between Kim Jong Un and Dennis Rodman is a test of patience for traditional public diplomacy practitioners who are often eager to be present at the policy planning level and not subject to the whims and musings of non-foreign policy experts who nevertheless shape foreign policy outcomes.[136] Said one former State Department official: "There is nobody at the CIA who can tell you more personally about Kim Jong Un than Dennis Rodman, and that in itself is scary."[137]

A case where such State Department officials were not openly present to shape policy in support of public attitudes was the border raid by the U.S. into Abbottabad, Pakistan to kill Osama Bin Laden. The Pakistani people condemned the covert operation,[138] but public opinion toward the U.S. was already so poor that a U.S. public diplomacy campaign to contextualize the policy would have been ineffective and, given the nature of the operation, of course impossible.[139]

Much of the public face of public diplomacy–how the concept became more recognized in the public consciousness–is attributed to the post-9/11 era that included a U.S.-led invasion of Afghanistan in October 2011, a war with Iraq in March 2003, and a Global War on Terror (GWOT) counter-terrorism strategy initiated by Republican President George W. Bush and reconstituted by a new Democratic president who heralded transparency and the winding down of two major wars in Asia. Obama very ceremoniously dropped the moniker "war on terror" at the start of his first term in office, part of a new counterterrorism strategy that chose a retail approach to terrorist networks over a nation-state approach.[140]

Bush placed the post-9/11 "new normal" in Cold War and World War II dimensions. He played big stick politics. He was going to end the war on terrorism in American terms. His September 20, 2001 speech to a joint session of Congress just nine days after September 11, 2001, made clear that the global war on terror would be a long, protracted war to which Americans would have to give full allegiance and personal sacrifice, just like generations had before them. "Our war on terror begins with al-Qaeda, but it does not end there." The president invoked variations on terror or terrorism 18 more times in his speech. During his State of the Union Address on January 29, 2002, Bush said that the U.S.-led war on terror would extend its reach to target the "Axis of Evil" countries of North Korea, Iran, Iraq, as well as enemies of America such as Hamas and Hezbollah.[141] This was definitely not "small ball" foreign policy, but what would become later labeled, albeit briefly, as a "global struggle against violent extremism."[142]

When Barack Obama took office in January 2009, the U.S. economy was in turmoil and the American public had counterterrorism fatigue after two protracted wars. Obama's focus was less ideological, less binary, and more practical. In his First Inaugural Address on January 20th, he pledged a new path for U.S. public diplomacy: "On this day, we gather because we have chosen hope over fear, unity of purpose over conflict and discord. On this day, we come to proclaim an end to the petty grievances and false promises, the recriminations and worn-out dogmas that for far too long have strangled our politics...To the Muslim world, we seek a new way forward, based on mutual interest and mutual respect. To those leaders around the globe who seek to sow conflict, or blame their society's ills on the West, know that your people will judge you on what you can build, not what you destroy. "[143] Such words were directed at not only the Bush administration's failed policies of division, but also as a sign of a new global commitment to repairing damaged international relations.

While Bush's public diplomacy profile was ideological and shaped by looking back, Obama's was pragmatic and shaped by looking forward. A precept of the Obama doctrine vis-à-vis public diplomacy is dialogue over quick action. Obama the presidential candidate was ridiculed for his oft-mentioned pledge to talk to our adversaries without preconditions. Not only did conservative Republicans predictably question this approach, but also his former Democratic opponent and later Secretary of State Hillary Clinton considered this pledge dangerous and wrong. Senator Obama's response to this attack was to telegraph a message as to how his presidency would break with the past: "I do think that there's a substantive difference between myself and Senator Clinton when it comes to meeting with our adversaries. I think that strong countries and strong presidents meet and talk with our adversaries. We shouldn't be afraid to do so. And that is that we should describe for the American people both in presidential debates, as well as president, what our foreign policy is and what we're going to do. [...] And it is my belief that we need a fundamental change if we're going to dig ourselves out of the hole that George Bush has placed us in. And that's going to require the kind of aggressive diplomacy. [...] That is ultimately going to make us safer. We've tried the other way. It didn't work."[144] Obama told West Point cadets not so much what he would do but what he wouldn't do in his foreign policy commitments. The U.S. would no longer "set goals that go beyond our responsibility, our means or our interests."[145] To neo-conservatives from the Bush years that were used to thinking in terms of limitless ideological struggles between good and evil, this must have come across as the decline of American civilization.

Public diplomacy during the two terms of George W. Bush held a prominent place if one views its role as integral to psychological and information warfare outcomes and not to mutual understanding outcomes proposed by his successor. Under Bush (and after the demise of USIA in 1999), the Department of Defense was the driving force for public diplomacy campaigns, not the Department of State. During the Bush years, DOD had the resources, while DOS had the public diplomacy legacy.[146] The term, "war on terror," was more appealing to the domestic American audience and widely condemned overseas. For the most part the U.S. public accepted the president's rhetorical broad brush, whose goal was to capture or kill enemies of America in particular and the West in general. Such binary thinking works well to unify a domestic population since battle lines are clear: moderates versus extremists, good versus evil. But such thinking leads to blurred lines between radical Islamic extremists and followers of Islam.

As the main face of the war on terrorism, President Bush was not the best messenger to try to delineate the religion of Islam from Islamic terrorists.[147] Further, the U.S. military complicated the open advocacy legacy of public diplomacy with the creation of clandestine offices like the Office of Strategic Influence that proposed a black propaganda program to influence global media coverage of the war on terror.[148] The Nuclear Posture Review of 2002 called on the Pentagon to draft contingency plans for the use of nuclear weapons against at least seven countries: Russia and the Axis of Evil (Iraq,

Iran, and North Korea) along with China, Libya and Syria."[149] This posture, leaked to the *Los Angeles Times*, dramatically shifted nuclear security strategy from the Cold War Mutual Assured Destruction (MAD) to Unilateral Assured Destruction (UAD). Bush's "go it alone" style overshadowed the collaborative possibilities of national security around issues of energy security or global efforts to prevent terrorism. Global resentment to Bush administration policies, coupled with two invasions of Muslim-majority countries, perpetuated anti-American attitudes and stymied efforts to address collective security and mutual understanding outcomes. In contrast, Obama's 2010 National Security Strategy emphasized a refreshed and renewed post-Bush engagement strategy with global publics:

> The United States Government will make a sustained effort to engage civil society and citizens and facilitate increased connections among the American people and peoples around the world—through efforts ranging from public service and educational exchanges, to increased commerce and private sector partnerships. In many instances, these modes of engagement have a powerful and enduring impact beyond our borders, and are a cost-effective way of projecting a positive vision of American leadership.[150]

This is not to suggest that all went well with Obama's new public diplomacy. Obama's first overseas speech, "A New Beginning," delivered on June 4, 2009, in Cairo, Egypt, was truly inspiring at the time with its cultural sensitivity and long list of promises, including closing the Guantanamo Bay Detention Facility, promoting a two-state solution, and supporting the advancement of democracy and human rights "everywhere."[151] In hindsight, the Cairo speech promised too much and created a say-do gap in US-Middle East relations. All of Obama's promises I've previously listed were unfulfilled. Further, U.S. favorability in Egypt declined from 2009-2010 by 17%, according to one Pew Global Attitudes survey.[152]

I have shared some public diplomacy differences between the Bush-Cheney administration and the Obama-Biden administration. Both Republican and Democratic administrations made mistakes in international communication and international relations that can serve as lessons for this region. And I believe that failures are essential steps for success so my critique here is not to complain but to instruct. Let me put these differences in context with specific lessons for the East Asian region.

Lesson One: Make Public Diplomacy a Mutual Understanding Process

President Bush's major mistake after 9/11 was to fuse public diplomacy with strictly America's national interest. Just like much of his either-or rhetoric, national security was cast in an either-or strategy. So-called targets of influence, the Afghani and Iraqi people, whose "winning hearts and minds" were integral to better U.S. relations with the Islamic world, were put in a terrible position of having one option: to support the U.S. foreign policy way that favored America's security or risk being aligned with enemy combatants. We all know that public diplomacy is a most important element of any nation's security. But when national leaders signal that a nation's security is more important than engagement or listening to the perspectives of global publics, it creates an atmosphere of distrust. Take, for example, the invasion of Iraq in March 2003. The Bush administration miscalculated that the Iraqi people so loathed Saddam Hussein that they would naturally pivot their allegiance of support to U.S. liberation from this dictator. But the two are mutually exclusive. The Iraqi people surely did not popularly support Hussein, but that didn't mean that they supported the U.S. invasion. The Bush team labeled the invasion "liberation" while the Iraqi people perceived it as an "occupation." The expected goodwill that the White House expected from the invasion was a major mistake.

What could the White House have done differently? A fundamental principle in public diplomacy and, for that matter, in intercultural communication, is to never presume anything. The U.S. should have understood that the Iraqi people harbored resentment toward the U.S. going back to Gulf War I when George Herbert

Walker Bush did not support the Shia uprising to rid Iraq of Hussein permanently. They felt exploited then and again in 2003. The Iraqi people's feeling of abandonment for the sake of protecting the lives of U.S. soldiers in 1991 was not properly acknowledged in the context of the 2003 invasion.

One of the reasons that nations do not take a mutual understanding, active listening approach to public diplomacy is because it is time-consuming and long-term. Much of public diplomacy plays out in urgent crisis situations but the day-to-day process of public diplomacy involves peace and conflict resolution and mediation. It does not occur on the front lines of conflict but rather in the everyday way that nations and their people communicate with each other. The East Asian region can learn from the U.S. superpower tendency to dictate more often than we listen. A dictatorial player in this region may be heard but very soon people will tune out the noise. A more reasoned, collaborative, and measured player will generate the goodwill needed for the long-term.

Lesson Two: Stop the Revolving Door and Stay Focused

This second lesson applies specifically to the Asia-Pacific or East Asian region and involves the structural organization of public diplomacy. Both Bush and Obama have not done an effective job of streamlining public diplomacy into the executive policy making process. In order to enact a more effective nation-branding program, you must have adequate resources that help raise the profile of public diplomacy in the eyes of the general population. The greatest public diplomacy asset that any nation has is its people, not the government, but governments are often the financiers of public diplomacy, which creates a viscous cycle of under-financing, under-resourcing, and under-leadership amidst rising expectations.

At the very top of the organizational structure we have an Under Secretary of State for Public Diplomacy and Public Affairs, sometimes referred to as "chief propagandist" or "public diplomacy czar." Since 1999, when USIA was abolished as an independent foreign affairs agency of the U.S. Government and merged into the

Department of State, this high-profile public diplomacy position has been empty for almost one-third of the time. There have been seven people in this position, six women and one man, since 1999. Tenures have been short, on average less than a year, and this much turnover and absenteeism suggests a lack of seriousness about this position from both the executive and legislative branches and a sense of not being able to make much of a difference for those serving in this position. I've written about two of the highest profile appointees, former top advertising executive, Charlotte Beers, and former Bush top communications adviser, Karen Hughes. [153] Charlotte Beers departed due to a reported illness just before the war in Iraq began and Karen Hughes left once in 2002 and again in 2007 to return to her family in Texas. Citing family reasons is a familiar refrain for a person who feels overworked or frustrated. Upon announcing her departure from her public diplomacy position in 2007, Hughes said that improving the U.S. image in the world was a "long-term challenge" that will outlast her tenure by years.[154] Indeed it is.

Clearly the U.S. example to the Asia-Pacific region is that leadership must be continual in order to address the following: What is the main message or messages that your nation is trying to convey to the region and the world? How do you connect such messaging to policies that are consistent with your country's ideals and that enhance your country's security? A revolving door of leadership at the top will not help to answer these core questions.

Lesson Three: Let Public Figures Lead the Conversation

Here is some straight talk about public diplomacy in an age of globalization. We aren't bereft of messages or nation-branding campaigns. Words and images proliferate. What is lacking is mindful attention to such messages. Global attention deficit is a consequence of the global information revolution. George Washington University Professor Bruce Gregory has said, "Attention—not information—is today's scarce resource."[155] Further, amidst all this competition for a person's attention in an environment of limited attention spans governments are not the best communicators. Global publics today trust their peers more than government leaders, and this applies most everywhere. Try as any government might, it will never be able to match the nimbleness and instantaneous nature of today's cheap, widely available communications technology that makes everyone a potential agitator, journalist, advocate, or teacher.

Even celebrities are public diplomats. Dennis Rodman is a bad example but Lady Gaga is a good example, at least her performance in the aftermath of 3/11. The U.S. has a very long history of using star power to advance diplomatic interests. We are, after all, the creators of the modern mass persuasion industries: advertising, mass popular entertainment through film and television, public relations, and marketing. But even long before these late 19th and early 20th century industries, we had our first celebrity public diplomat, Benjamin Franklin, who charmed the French Court and King Louis XVI. Now what could Lady Gaga do for Japan in 2011? She was not formally trained in diplomacy and this was to her advantage. She didn't apprentice or study diplomatic textbooks. She has an "it" quality that resonates. Famous people who serve, unintentionally or not as public diplomats, come across best when they seem unrehearsed but moved to act. And this is why I focused particularly on Lady Gaga's message following 3/11. Not only that, but in 2012 the U.S. government asked me to address her public diplomacy skills set in several university talks across Japan as a State Department-sponsored Speaker and Specialist with the United States Embassy in Tokyo.

Gaga's message to Japan was easily translatable, anything but formally diplomatic, very personal, even colloquial in tone. It is precisely the non-diplomatic style, or, her citizen diplomacy style, that made her appealing. She referred to Video Music Aid Japan as "a perfect way to bridge culture with philanthropy." The Haus of Gaga creative team designed "Pray for Japan" wristbands the day of the disaster and raised over $3 million. Her diplomatic message is her belief in the power of music, not necessarily her music but anyone's music, to change people's lives. Her simple message was "Japan is very safe. I'm running around eating Shabu-shabu. The most important thing we could do right now is boost tourism. Come to Japan and enjoy the beautiful country." These words could fit on any bumper sticker or poster. Were these words shared by former Secretary of State Hillary Clinton they would not have been received the same. In fact, they would have placed an official diplomat in the uncomfortable and unexpected role of commercial huckster.

The Secretary of State is our highest-level diplomat whose role is to improve international relations, be they political, economic, or cultural, between the U.S. and the world. The Secretary of State is not the Secretary of Commerce, however. Formal diplomats are limited in scope in how they can present both the content and presentation of their messages to overseas publics. Celebrities have no such restrictions. Had Gaga said something outrageous in language or decorum, she still would have been on balance well received because she reached tens of millions, if not hundreds of millions of people with her message. Of course, the Internet mass outreach with its Facebook and Twitter dominance is a two-edged sword. The Department of State swiftly withdrew a planned International Woman of Courage Award for Egyptian activist, Samira Ibrahim, who tweeted anti-American and anti-Semitic statements on her Twitter account.[156]

Now here is something else to consider. The State Department's official Twitter account (@StateDept) has, as of April 2016, over 2.46 million followers. Lady Gaga (@LadyGaga) has over 58 million followers, of which I am a lowly one. With few exceptions in America (Bill Clinton, Barack Obama) no government official or government website can compare to the global reach of certain popular culture celebrities. Gaga has extraordinary media savvy. She is not formally trained in persuasion or propaganda, but she understands the good propaganda outreach of her platforms that include marriage equality, AIDS research, and global disaster relief. Celebrity platforms bring three things: (a) immediate access to local, national and global media as well as the ability to generate huge "buzz" through social media; (b) access to world leaders; which in turn leads to (c) resources (donations, raising awareness about safety issues). Celebrities like Gaga are not visiting Japan in a formal context as traditional diplomats. They are not representing the

American people or a specific constituency. Nevertheless, they are public diplomats because we are now in an age when anyone can potentially be a diplomat. Gone are the days when only representatives of states or governments were diplomats.

Lesson Four: Embrace Social Media and Media for the Masses

In 2010 I called the new Obama-era public diplomacy "Lady Gaga in a NATO cap." At a gathering of both military and State Department officials at the National Summit of Strategic Communication in Washington, DC, I wondered aloud if someone like a Lady Gaga was representative of a cultural shift in how we're now bringing attention to global governance issues. At the time Gaga was openly acknowledging her support for the 82nd Airborne American troops in Afghanistan who did a YouTube spoof of her "Telephone" video. The video was praised by military brass as offering a window into how some troops unwind in a stressful warzone. The spontaneity of the video worked to the military brass advantage.

The lessons for the East Asian region are many. Government officials need to model the shift in behavior among Department of State and Department of Defense officials who now embrace global publics in a diverse and comprehensive way. When I worked at the U.S. Information Agency from 1992-1994, the Internet was still brand new for us. The diplomatic playbook vis-à-vis public diplomacy was largely an intergovernmental policy process. The old way of doing public diplomacy was to share select information with select elite publics in the government's interest. The government to mass public model wasn't as common. Today, it's much more a free-for-all and grab bag of information exchange with the power of visual media and storytelling through trendy sound bites or 140 characters. It's very difficult for government bureaucrats to keep up with private industry or even children born into the social media era, some of whom master an iPad and iPhone as tykes.

The new way of doing public diplomacy is to share more information with the masses. The mass citizenry is engaged more by public figures with mass appeal. Some of that engagement is low-brow entertainment, but it does have influence in how much mind space it occupies. Traditional diplomats think in terms of select or target audiences. Lady Gaga, Bono, and Justin Bieber think in terms of global audiences. Their fan base knows no national boundary. Their message is universal, not nation-specific, although in Gaga's case, she tailored her message to helping rebuild Japan through global tourism. Celebrity public diplomats operate on a platform in the NGO (nongovernmental) sphere and are more likely to be found in the emerging noosphere (mind space) that captures hearts and minds with transcendent messages of peace, human rights, and human dignity.

Not everyone will embrace the rise of celebrity diplomacy. It is healthy to be skeptical. Many argue that the rich and famous are parachute diplomats who fly in first class and reach audiences that lifelong professional diplomats and relief workers couldn't reach in a lifetime. So why celebrate the celebrity in diplomacy? It all comes down to focusing attention. There is no more powerful picture of food safety after 3/11 than Lady Gaga sipping tea in a "Pray for Japan" teacup in Tokyo. Her demonstration of safety served as a form of cultural mediation: a mega star of planet earth serving as a bridge between mass society and institutions that are conditioned toward elite targets.

Lesson Five: Play to Your Strengths (But Be Open to New Challenges)

The East Asian and Asian-Pacific region commands a lot of the world's attention these days as an economic powerhouse; the Association of Southeast Asian Nations alone represents in GDP alone the world's tenth largest economy. You also have the world's second and third largest economies along with Hong Kong with its leading financial markets and Singapore with its top ranking in public trust of politicians.[157] It makes for crowded space when it comes to marketing one's nation.

My suggestion is to go with what your country is known for and make it stronger. Japan is a cultural diplomacy superpower. The Japan Foundation was established in 1972 for this very purpose. We have no such equivalent in the United States since the U.S. Information Agency was rolled into the Department of State in 1999. Even if someone has never traveled here, he can recognize the cultural distinctiveness of the country in many forms: karaoke, sushi, futon, manga, anime, J-Pop, J-Fashion, traditional culture (rock garden, Zen architecture, tea ceremony, Kimono culture, ikebana). Karaoke, according to Japan's Cultural Affairs Agency, is the most practiced cultural activity in the nation. A natural offspring of the Cool Japan vision is the AKB48 girl group (Akihabara 48), not only in Japan but also through spin-off versions throughout the region. The popular song and dance act is now being enlisted in the sale of "reconstruction bonds." Japan has held cultural appeal for quite some time. Before Hello Kitty, Doraemon (the earless robot cat), or Pokemon, there was Astro Boy and Godzilla. The difference between then and now is that the J-state is finally taking notice that J-pop has J-policy links.

The problem with Cool Japan is that what it means to be cool is ephemeral. Yesterday's Cool Japan is tomorrow's Cool Korea or Cool India. Every nation in the region has its "cool" aspects. The Japanese government and institutions like the Japan Foundation recognize that being a cultural superpower isn't enough, especially against the backdrop of the lost decades. Nevertheless, the emphasis on culture continues in a region where China, Korea and Taiwan assert their own cultural features, China in particular with its global Confucius Institutes. The question remains: Is culture power in the Asian-Pacific region just politics by other means? Protracted island disputes fueled by hot rhetoric and displays of bravado on the seas overshadow anything cool. As Senator J. William Fulbright said in a 1983 speech to the Council on International Educational Exchange:

Educational exchange can turn nations into people, contributing as no other form of communication can to the humanizing of international relations. Man's capacity for decent behavior seems to vary directly with his perception of others as individual humans with human motives and feelings, whereas his capacity for barbarism seems related to his perception of an adversary in abstract terms, as the embodiment, that is, of some evil design or ideology.

The enthusiasm for the U.S. century with its bipolar fixation (Cold War, War on Terror) is waning while interest in the rise of an Asian multipolar system is waxing. I have shared some of the challenges with my own country's public diplomacy in the last two administrations. What I foresee in this region is a growth industry in nation branding, place branding (Seoul, Tokyo, Hong Kong, Singapore), and regional branding (Asian Century, Asian educational and cultural exchanges). There will be challenges ahead, mostly revolving around funding and leadership. How will Asia-Pacific globalize its curriculum to attract more foreign students? Right now the region is the biggest "supplier" of international students to the OECD countries. More recently, Malaysia, Singapore and China have committed resources to creating a "world-class" education system with more English-language courses and inexpensive tuition fees. As a result, international students are coming.[158] I mention international educational exchange as my last point because my entire experience with Japan has been as a sponsored exchange professional (twice with USIA in 1993, 1994), 2010 (Department of State) and 2012 (Fulbright Program). I've been on two Fulbright scholarships and am privileged to say that I knew Senator Fulbright and continue to have contact with his widow, Harriet Mayer Fulbright.

The best opportunity for long-term attitudinal shifts toward a place comes from person-to-person contact in a setting of mutual trust and understanding. Note that I didn't say guarantee but rather opportunity. Exchange outcomes vary, but we have enough research on record to point to support for better outcomes, not only in personal development but also in establishment of multicultural social networks.[159] Cultural and educational exchange is the cornerstone of U.S. public diplomacy, despite the fact that the Department of State spends half of its funding on international broadcasting activities. Mass media exposure alone is a poor predictor of changes in attitudes, but if combined with person-to-person exposure, then attitude shifts in a positive direction are more likely. This is why the Fulbright program for the U.S. is still the gold standard. The UK hosts the Rhodes Scholars from the United States, which number 32, but the U.S. sends over 1,100 Fulbright Scholars to 125 countries, and hosts 800 foreign scholars from 95 countries. Overall, the Fulbright program is active in 155 countries. My vision for the Asia-Pacific region is that it will establish its own regional brand of exchanges modeled on the success of the Fulbright program. From this it is possible to envision more cooperation and collaboration in other areas: peace, security, development, healthcare, and the environment.

PART II.
PERSPECTIVES
ON JAPAN'S
SOFT POWER

WOMEN'S EMPOWERMENT

THE TIME IS NOW, JAPAN

I have proof that Japan is making progress in women's empowerment. But it doesn't just come from the global economic and political agenda priority item known as "Advancing Women's Empowerment and Gender Equality."

The Group of Seven summit at Ise-Shima was a success for women through random acts of kindness on display, besides the fact that empowering women in Japan and around the world has become a logic-driven position and not just a feel-good emotion.

Empowering women is good for economic development. We should have more capable women in positions of power. It's not rocket science. It's sandbox sensibility. But enough about an agenda item. Let me share the unsung women leaders I met.

I wasn't with the designated big league G-7 leaders, otherwise known as all those men plus German Chancellor Angela Merkel, but I did have an opportunity to access the International Media Center near where those leaders were meeting.

My thank you list begins with the young women who so capably escorted me and many other visitors, VIPs and the world's media through the Japan Exhibition annex. This was an extraordinary display of Japan's innovation and tradition, but what made it come alive were the bilingual women volunteers on hand to converse about what one was seeing. The women who escorted me were bright university students, some from Mie Prefecture, one an exchange student from Taiwan. Without them I would have felt like that aimless shopper who says, "I'm just looking," and departs quietly shortly after.

Another random act of women's leadership came from an Ise-Shima Summit volunteer at Mikimoto Pearl Island, located in Toba City, Mie Prefecture. An excited group of local residents, Ama divers and Taiko performers was waiting for the arrival of first lady Akie Abe, and her G-7 partners Joachim Sauer, husband of Germany's chancellor; Sophie Gregoire-Trudeau, wife of the Canadian prime minister; and Małgorzata Tusk, spouse of the European Council president.

By now I had been on my feet for hours and was feeling quite peaked. My phone battery had died, my camera battery was weak, and my body was weaker. Within minutes of arriving, a volunteer asked what she could do for me. I'm sure she could see that a number of batteries, as well as myself, needed recharging. She found electricity and gave me her chilled tea.

I designated her my summit star volunteer and asked her where should I send a letter of thanks. She responded, "I'm just a housewife from Nagoya." I laughed and said, "Drop the word 'just' before 'a housewife' in your vocabulary. You are making a big difference to me as a citizen ambassador for Japan."

Then I asked, "How did you get here? What is your story?" She applied as a volunteer in answer to an ad and received both English and hospitality training. And where did my star volunteer end up? Serving as a translator to the G-7 spouses as they graciously worked the line to greet the Ama divers and local residents.

Another vivid memory involves Sophie Gregoire-Trudeau embracing a young Japanese girl who had just performed for Japan's first lady and the other VIPs. The girl had greeted Canada's first lady and Akie Abe, and burst into tears of excitement. The heartfelt moment caused several Japanese reporters to rush over for an on-the-spot interview with the new media star, who undoubtedly said that it was a thrill to present Toba to the world.

Young and old, international and homegrown, women were making a difference, taking the initiative, sharing the conversation, giving a hug of encouragement and comfort. And Joachim Sauer, a quantum chemist professor, was right at home with the women spouses, taking the time to give the Mie Prefecture local residents a lifelong memory.

Louisa May Alcott, author of the classic *Little Women*, said in the 19th century, "I only ask for a chance to be a useful, happy woman, and I don't think that is a bad ambition." Nearly a century and a half later, we are still asking for that same chance.

The Amaterasu Omikami spirit prevailed from watching Akie Abe engage with the other G-7 spouses along the Isuzu river's edge at Ise Jingu, to the Ama divers displaying their skills before the VIPs, to the young women volunteers at the Japan Exhibition moving from topics that ranged from the world's thinnest and refined silk, made in Japan, to "Hobalin," an underwater drone used for deep-sea exploration.

Don't we want women to shine here in Japan and elsewhere with the kind of compassion, care and concern that I experienced during such a high-profile event? The men may still be overwhelmingly in charge but capable women seem to be in control of making everything flow smoothly.

While so much of the news reports continue to focus on the negative — the declining GDP growth — I can't help but see the positive: the rise in gross domestic power of the feminine persuasion. And if I were planning the hospitality committee for Tokyo 2020, there's this housewife I know from Nagoya.

The Japan Times, June 7, 2016

ISE JINGU: TELLING JAPAN'S STORY TO THE REST OF THE WORLD

The Japanese people are world famous for their love of *sakura*, the symbol of spring. Spread out your blankets, open up the picnic baskets and pop the corks: the cherry blossoms are a feast for the senses. As with any beauty, the petals cannot sustain their head-turning quotient for more than a few weeks, after which we watch them dance in the wind and carpet our walkways.

It is this fleeting season of *hanami* that is perhaps the most recognized symbol of Japan and its reverence and respect for nature. Another tradition deserves its place in Japan's storytelling to the world: Ise Jingu (officially known as "Jingu") and its 20-year ritual known as Shikinen Sengu (shrine reconstruction ceremony), passed down across generations for over 1,300 years. The first Sengu was performed in 690 and the 62nd was conducted in 2013.

This year's Group of Seven summit (Ise-Shima summit) is taking place on Kashikojima island in Mie Prefecture. Central Japan was chosen to allow the world's top leaders to have firsthand experience with Japan's nature, core culture and traditions. Ise Jingu has much to share about sustainability and continuity that could help shape the conversation of the global influentials. But to begin to know it, you must visit. Picture books cannot tell the full story, for all the senses must be fully engaged. It is why Shinto and Ise Jingu are called the "soul of Japan."

During my initial visit to Ise Jingu, a Shinto priest beckoned me to walk around this sacred space, no small feat for the feet. The land area of Jingu is comparable to the size of Paris. Shinto is a practice without scriptures, a founder, or a doctrine, although it is informed by Japanese myths recorded in "Kojiki" and "Nihon-Shoki" ancient history books. The priest did not want to explain the meaning of Shinto or the shrine as much as encourage me to just be present in the moment. I began to think of Jimi Hendrix. Ah, the experience. In feeling this moment, you begin to know Shinto philosophy, to see everything in the world as sacred as expressed through deities called kami.

"Just go out and feel it," he said. And so I did.

I walked. I listened to the crunch of my feet on the stone path and the song of birds. I noted the forest green shimmering moss and the artistry of fern patterns on rocks. I marveled at the crowds of people of all ages crossing the Ujibashi Bridge, giving an exit bow at the Torii main gate that separates the material world, Ise City, from the spirit world of Jingu. When I performed a kami prayer, a gust of wind lifted up the white curtain (Mitobari) like a giant hand and gave a fleeting but full glimpse of the Kotaijingu (Naiku), the main sanctuary dedicated to the female guardian of Japan and the Imperial family, the vigorous spirit known as Amaterasu-Omikami.

In the scent of the Japanese cypress and the flowing current of the Isuzugawa river, you couldn't help but feel a sense of rejuvenation and the chains of life that unite us. Yes, life is short, but there is comfort at knowing that some part of you lives on in your legacy, how you have lived, who you have influenced, and who has influenced you, including family and ancestors.

The Japanese love and respect for nature — its bounty, its delicacy, its furor — is throughout Jingu. Nature is a great teacher and the ultimate influencer. The divine is all of life and its treasures: rocks, trees, stones, wind, sun, moon, mountains, persons, those that inspire, educate, provide, and guide. The kami give us a sense of ceaseless wonder. It brings to mind the expansive mentoring system here with senpai and sensei in present and ancestors from past, who provide instruction for our actions, attitude, and decision-making.

The spiritual essence of Japan, as shown through my visit to Ise Jingu, is its agriculturally rich history where people had to rely on the natural resources of pollinating wind and ample water to sustain its rice culture.

Rice meant life. If everyone worked together, the nation would survive and thrive. For shelter, there was wood from this heavily forested country, before the industrial period brought in the steel and concrete.

Wood, like life, does not last forever. It cannot endure. It falls into deterioration and decay. It must be regrown and rebuilt. Each time a rebuild occurs, traditions are maintained and the artisan spirit thrives. In the impermanence of wood and the fragility of rice cultivation, we rely on our generational knowledge to sustain us.

Is there a Shinto and Ise Jingu message for the global leaders who will come together in Mie Prefecture this spring? Yes, indeed. Yukichi Fukuzawa said, "The world is large." Global problems are large and looming, but the resolutions are small if we all learn to like and respect each other enough to work together to resolve them.

Fundamentally we all want more happiness than sorrow. We seek protective shelter, a good harvest, and a hope for the future that life will go on long after our lives end here on earth.

At Ise Jingu, the 20-year ritual of Shikinen Sengu is a ritual of the past thousand years to inform the present. There is no time like the present to show gratitude to nature's bounty and direct our human powers of ingenuity to recycle, reuse, and repair to mutual dependence, the essential spirit of Japan.

The Japan Times, March 21, 2016

THE FATE OF A DOLPHIN ACTIVIST IN JAPAN'S FLAWED DEMOCRACY

What do dolphins, David Bowie and *The Economist* have in common? Freedom. Dolphins seek freedom. Bowie, who loved Japan and Japan loved him, represents the freedom to express yourself. Bowie gave permission for his song "Heroes" to be used in the Oscar-winning documentary "The Cove," about the dolphin hunt in Taiji, Wakayama Prefecture.

The Economist is in search of more freedom, especially in Japan's political landscape. The Economist Democracy Index 2015 demoted Japan from a full democracy to a flawed democracy, along with Costa Rica, South Korea and France. The report from the Economist Intelligence Institute cites "Japan's increasing media censorship" since the State Secrets Law went into effect December 2014 and "evidence of the ruling Liberal Democratic Party's (LDP) pressuring firms to withhold advertising in unfavored publications, were enough to push the country's score below the 8.00 threshold, meaning that the country is now classified in our Democracy Index as a 'flawed democracy.' "

British understatement represents this media censorship as rationale for Japan's democracy decline. The Japanese government seems at times afraid of its own global relations shadow, or the shadow of any dissenting point of view.

Take the case of 76-year-old dolphin activist, Ric O'Barry, star of "The Cove." He is now starring in another real time documentary after landing at Tokyo's Narita airport on Jan. 18. The Japanese Ministry of Justice filed an order for his deportation on Jan. 21, the same day that the Democracy Index 2015 was released. The charges against O'Barry involve falsely representing the purpose of his visit. His son, Lincoln O'Barry, states his father's purpose quite clearly: "He has been working for 13 years to expose the brutal dolphin hunt there, and this is their latest attempt to shut him out."

The government of Japan has a right to deny entry to anyone it wishes. And the government of Japan can build its deportation case against O'Barry, who at some point will be ordered out of Japan. We all are guests at the invitation of the host country and our stay as guests is a privilege, not a right. But lost in this process is an opportunity for greater understanding.

The global press and social media echo chamber leads with headlines like this: "Japan to Dolphin Activist: Get Out" and "Flipper Trainer Detained in Japan." Viral petitions are circulating for O'Barry's release. While there is plenty of sympathy for O'Barry's detainment, there is little sympathy for the Japanese government, even if O'Barry misrepresented the purpose of his visit. His tourist habits suggest he wasn't here for the Kyary Pamyu Pamyu attraction at Universal Cool Japan 2016.

Contrast the holding pattern of O'Barry to an open protest in another flawed democracy, France. The same week that O'Barry had the door to Japan's democracy closed to him, the deputy minister of ecology Laurence Abeille welcomed animal rights activist and former "Baywatch babe" Pamela Anderson, who spoke in France's National Assembly against the force-feeding of ducks and geese for the highly popular cuisine delicacy foie gras.

The Canadian-born celebrity Anderson took her inspiration to speak directly to the French government and its citizens from French actress Bridget Bardot, who came to Canada in the late 1970s to protest another Trudeau government and its slaughtering of baby seals. A pro foie-gras organization called Anderson's visit a "publicity stunt" by "an American TV star from the eighties" who condemned "a jewel in the crown of gastronomy and French culture."

True to that last point. Everything in this social media society is publicity-driven. That didn't stop Anderson from accepting a government minister's invitation to speak, making her point, and going home to her adopted home America. Conversely, it is hard to imagine a Japanese minister of anything extending an invitation to O'Barry to speak in the Diet.

Whatever the immigration outcome of O'Barry, he has already won in the courtroom of public opinion. Global public sympathy is on his side, whereas Japan looks overly sensitive on this contentious issue of dolphin hunting.

There is something that the government of Japan could do to even the playing field in making its case to the world. Don't let O'Barry leave Japan without inviting him to a well-publicized debate at the University of Tokyo. Have him go up against the most seasoned advocates for continuing the dolphin hunt in Taiji. Invite the Japanese and foreign media to cover the debate gavel-to-gavel, and include live tweeting and a live stream version for the world to tune in. Add a focus group to the mix, consisting of pro- and anti-activists along with the undecided. Vote on a debate winner.

The winner would be democratic freedom of expression. It would show the world that Japan's top-ranked institution of higher learning is not shy about debating one of the most contentious policies impacting Japan's relations with the world. The event itself will not settle the debate about dolphins, but it might mute the growing chorus of people that views Japan as the democracy where dissent is in detention.

The Japan Times, January 26, 2016

JAPAN'S FUTURE IS AN OISTER

If I told you that Japan had a world-class science and technology university that could one day stand tall among the big trees of MIT or Stanford, could you guess its name and where it's located? Hint: It's not in Honshu, home to Japan's top name-brand national universities like the University of Tokyo and Kyoto University. This university is about 640 km from the rest of Japan and even further away in mission and philosophy.

Call it where science and technology in subtropical paradise meets some of the world's best lab-based problem solvers. Okinawa Institute of Science and Technology Graduate University (OIST) is the best university you've likely never heard of in Japan.

Its reputation and academic style adhere to no national boundaries. It's not typically Japanese or Western: it is an open campus — the Okinawan people are welcome to drop by or attend Open Campus community fairs. It offers 24-hour Open Labs where scientists are encouraged to share equipment, and it is collaborative and interdisciplinary in teaching, research and publishing.

Everyone, student and professor alike, is a research associate. In short, it's an academic dream, unless your ideal academic setting is a closed office door inside-the-silo mentality.

It is the most diverse international university that Japan has to offer, which is why some of the best science minds in the world keep responding. Eighty percent of the doctoral students come from overseas, many from the Asian region, but also from Europe, the United States and the United Kingdom. This year's incoming class of 24 is from 15 countries. Just 20 percent of the student body is from Japan.

The students I met were "user friendly" with their ability to explain neuroscience and molecular physics to this social scientist more comfortable in a class about politics and media. The OIST way is to make science and technology more accessible. It encourages its doctoral students to act more like professors who profess — to give public presentations and engage in public speaking as much as possible. Why else would an institution promote science in the global interest if it cannot communicate with the world?

English is the operating language of this Japanese university, which received a nearly $1 billion budget, including construction of the impressive campus, over 10 years from the Cabinet Office. It may seem highly incongruous with the Japanese-language dominance in the classroom elsewhere in Japan, but the smart visionaries behind OIST, including the president of the University of Tokyo, Dr. Akito Arima (1989-1993), knew that global English — the primary language of science, academic publishing and the Internet — would attract the world's best students and faculty. Any Japanese student who enrolls at OIST will be trained in science and technology that prepares that student for placement across the world.

Why does a Japanese university have just one 1 of 5 Japanese students? Part of it could be a certain intimidation to using English full time for research collaboration and presentation, but OIST offers English courses to all its students, and offers Japanese courses to its non-native Japanese.

Another reason may be declining interest in the natural sciences. A recent survey by the Japan Youth Research Institute showed that Japanese high school students registered the lowest interest in nature and science compared with their counterparts in China, South Korea and the United States. It's notable that China and South Korea start teaching students English as a second language in grade three (age 8) rather than the typical junior high level (age 12) in Japan.

Japan's education ministry has 200 high schools designated as "Super Science High Schools," so we know that the national interest is tied to hard science advancement, but if student interest overall is declining, then we have to think of better ways to entice young people to want to put on the lab coat and start experimenting.

Japan is world renowned for some of the best minds in science and technology. The results of Japan's junior high school students in mathematics and science remain consistently at an internationally top level, but in terms of personal interest in the subjects (degree of like/dislike), they are at some of the lowest levels internationally. OIST would like to have at least half Japanese students, if not more, but so far the tug of science in paradise lags behind the name-brand mainland universities.

OIST has the potential to serve as the model to how an innovative, entrepreneurial university can operate in Japan. The OIST spirit to innovate comes from a wild dream that might just be realizable — an Okinawan version of Silicon Valley next to a Stanford-like university in beauty and reputation.

The school must develop substantial financial independence within 10 years. Its future success depends on a business model shepherded by patents from scientific discoveries. The profits will be shared equally among the research associates (professor and student), the research laboratory and the university.

Japan continues to try to raise its global profile politically in an updated security regime and global trade through the Trans-Pacific Partnership, but it has a chronic problem in global education. Japan's top-ranked universities are losing global luster and fewer Japanese students are going abroad for undergraduate or postgraduate education. This, in turn, makes them less able to communicate well in English.

"We are living in a period of rapid change driven by science and technology. Japan has taken a very bold move in creating a high level graduate university that is adapted to the needs of the next leaders of international science and industry. It is a privilege to contribute," said OIST Acting President Albrecht Wagner.

"OIST is already a shining star for Japan in the highly competitive world of top-level science and technology universities. The dream of Okinawa as an international center of R&D is becoming a reality," enthused Robert Baughman, executive vice president for Sustainable Development of Okinawa, an OIST group.

What I witnessed at OIST were students from around the world serving as well-spoken, poised science and technology citizen ambassadors. They were proud to be OISTers, proud that it was a Japanese government-initiative and even prouder to serve the Okinawan community. Whatever they are doing at OIST is a bit magical and we need to spread some of that magic across the rest of

Japan so that the next time a young Japanese person is asked about his or her attitude toward science, the interest will match the ability.

The Japan Times, November 23, 2015

IN LIEU OF TAKING IN REFUGEES, ABE OPENS UP CHECKBOOK

Last year, 5,000 people applied for refugee status in Japan. 11 were accepted.

This past March, *The Economist* ran a headline, "No entry: As the world's refugee problem grows, Japan pulls up the drawbridge." The article included an image of the red circle (the sun) that is the flag symbol of Japan with a white bar through it, the symbol for "Do Not Enter" signs in Europe. This month, *The Washington Post* weighed in with an article headlined, "As Europe makes room for refugees, some in Japan ask why not us?"

Japan is a strong target for refugee criticism because of its modest engagement in social media and global communications. Typically, it doesn't proactively make its case to the world, largely allowing the international press and the Twitterverse to frame its issues for it.

The *Post* article, comparing the refugee response of Europe with Japan's closed doors, quotes heavily from Twitter messages that argue for opening the doors to refugees in Japan, including @robotopia, who wrote, "It's insane that Japan, which has enough abandoned homes to house all Syrian #refugees TWICE over, took in only 11 asylum seekers in 2014." The comment sparked a debate, including from me (@drpersuasion) about the feasibility to open abandoned houses in rural areas of Japan to refugees from Syria. GoodandbadJapan responded, "but they don't speak Japanese and might put the rubbish out on the wrong day."

Accepting refugees to Japan is not unprecedented, just very limited. Between 1978 and 2005, Japan accepted over 11,000 Indo-Chinese refugees fleeing the Vietnam conflict. Japan was the first Asian country in 2010 to participate in the United Nations High Commissioner for Refugees' resettlement program, a pilot program to bring 90 Myanmar refugees from Thailand over the course of three years. Other than Myanmar and the Indo-Chinese, the Japanese government doesn't have much experience in targeting a specific group for refugees to come to Japan, especially from a vastly different culture. Japan recognized 577 refugees from 1982 to 2010 under the 1981 Convention Relating to the Status of Refugees and the 1982 Protocol Relating to the Status of Refugees.

Where Japan shines is in providing assistance as a leading humanitarian nation. It is a top official development assistance (ODA) country, just below the United States, United Kingdom and Germany. International aid ostensibly greatly improves the lives of refugees. But because Japan is not a top host nation for refugees, it is vulnerable to critical global media stories singling it out as a rich country that takes in the least refugees. In contrast, Germany is celebrated for opening arms wide to take in up to half a million refugees. Germany may be facing incredible burdens from this population infusion, but its liberal refugee policy blowback may take years.

Germany was the Cinderella of the refugee crisis and Japan the Evil Stepmother before Abe's address to the United Nations on Sept. 29. Abe announced a tripling of the budget from last year to $810 million in assistance to refugees and internally displaced people in Syria and Iraq. He also announced $750 million "to help build peace and fully ensure this peace across the Middle East and Africa." But that is what Japan is doing "over there" and Japan may still be subjected to criticism for not taking in the most vulnerable publics fleeing conflict.

The refugee criticism of Japan risked threatening an image that Japanese leaders have attempted to cultivate in developing nation brand Japan as a compassionate leader in the world. One of Japan's most honored citizens, Madame Sadako Ogata, high commissioner of the U.N.'s refugee agency for a decade (1991-2000), remains one of the country's most honored citizens. At age 88, she remains president of the Japan International Cooperation Agency, a Tokyo-based developmental organization that works to alleviate poverty, as one mission.

The focus on Syria may also carry with it a bitter memory for many Japanese. This past January, Abe announced a $100 million donation to help the countries of the Middle East fighting Islamic State inside their borders. Within a few days, Muslim militants with

IS beheaded Kenji Goto, a journalist, and Haruna Yukawa, the Japanese hostage that Goto had gone to Syria to attempt to rescue.

Abe's tripling of humanitarian assistance for refugees and internally displaced people in the Middle East is notable. But there is a more recent bitter memory that remains, a population of internally displeased people who were opposed to the controversial security legislation passed just after midnight on Sept. 19. Abe's U.N. speech made passing reference to the collective self-defense measures that were defined by a brawl in the Diet and hundreds of thousands who took to the streets. The prime minister positively framed the security summer of discontent like a "Wish you were here" picture postcard.

Japan's security changes spell the end of a pacifist Constitution and Abe's glossing over of this reality in his U.N. speech is as telling as his positive public relations surrounding doing more for the most vulnerable publics in Syria and Iraq.

The Japan Times, October 4, 2015

THE ABE ADMINISTRATION'S ARROGANCE OF POWER MOMENT

On the cusp of the 70th anniversary of the end of World War II when Emperor Hirohito made his historic speech of surrender, the Abe government is attempting to drive through the Diet 11 security bills that will forever alter the landscape of Japan's postwar history. The nation that does not wage war will be no more if it gets its way.

Guided in its efforts is a military-industrial complex that is salivating to get Japan to share the burden of fighting with its closest ally, the United States. Japan has recently expressed interest in joining the North Atlantic Treaty Organization missile-building consortium, a move in seamless alliance with this New Normal for Japan, a normal that we believe threatens global security.

As scholars from Japan and the U.S., we oppose the new security bills and call on anyone who is unfamiliar with what's happening to get informed. What we have here is legislation without representation; at its worst, tyranny.

In clear violation of Article 9 of the Constitution, which famously renounces war as a sovereign right of the nation and the threat or use of force as a means of settling international disputes, these bills would provide for Japan's Self-Defense Forces to cooperate actively with U.S. and other foreign military operations overseas. If adopted, Japan will be able to use military force even when it is not attacked, under the name of collective self-defense. Let us not mince words: this spells the end of Article 9 without ever formally amending it according to due process of law.

We cannot believe any assurances from a prime minister who thinks nothing of the constitutional ban and popular opposition that these security bills will strictly limit Japan's military role. This legislation opens the door to virtually unfettered government discretion over the use of force that violates Japan's fundamental principle over six decades of an exclusively self-defense posture.

The Japanese people, having been the only population to suffer atomic bombs, are overwhelmingly in support of maintaining peaceful relations with the world. They wish to protect the sanctity and heritage of Article 9. A nation that renounces war is part of Japan's peace national brand, and has allowed Japan to develop as a world class economic and culture power with a strong mandate for humanitarian assistance, disaster relief and development aid.

Should these security bills get passed, Japan will no longer be able to advocate for a peace and nonviolence paradigm in national security. Our view is that Japan's peace Constitution should not be altered but should continue to serve as a model for other countries. It should certainly not be "reinterpreted" arbitrarily by the government of the day.

Article 23 of the Constitution guarantees academic freedom, and it is within this guarantee that we, as public scholars in Japan and signatories to the Association of Scholars Opposed to the Security-related Bills, are speaking out. One of us is an Abe fellow at Keio University and former Fulbright scholar at Sophia University; the other is a political scientist at Sophia University who received the Friend of the Free Press award this spring from the Foreign Correspondents' Club of Japan.

We stand with the growing political protests from scholars, students, lawyers, workers and mothers that are coalescing against a government displaying total disregard for democratic speech and assembly. Japan is the closest Asian ally to the U.S. and we take this binational alliance of democracies literally and to heart. We oppose this government fait accompli that refuses to listen to citizen debate, discussion, or dialogue. We call on the Abe government to observe the democratic and constitutional due process before it does irreparable damage to the national character of postwar Japan.

The Abe government has shown no concern for the Japanese people. It is attempting to circumvent the Constitution by ramming the security bills through the Diet without the constitutionally mandated process for a constitutional revision (Article 96) requiring a two-third majority of both houses of parliament and a majority support from the people in a special referendum.

We write, backed as we are from thousands of scholars and millions of Japanese who share our opposition, to object to the security bills in principle and process. Our objections are marinated with affection, concern and care for Japan and the Japanese people.

Prime Minister Shinzo Abe's administration cannot claim to have a popular mandate for imposing these changes, even if we leave aside the unconstitutionality of the bills. It has a large majority in both houses only because of record-high voting abstention rates, a divided opposition, a muzzled media, the bias of the first-past-the-post system, and the enormous disparity of the value of the vote that has been repeatedly ruled to be in a state of unconstitutionality by the courts. In reality, only one in four voters actively voted for Abe's Liberal Democratic Party. The prime minister has, nevertheless, said that within 20 to 30 years he will be vindicated; thus, public opinion, which he seems to view with disdain, is dismissed. We believe that the Japanese people deserve more credit and respect than what they are being shown by their government.

These security bills stand against Japan's well-deserved human security reputation in the world. Human security puts people's needs and rights first, and views security within the prism of a multidisciplinary understanding of the world that involves development studies, education, science and technology for good, and peaceful international relations.

The United Nation's Human Development Report of 1994 argues that global human security is about promoting "freedom from want" and "freedom from fear" for all people. With Japan's growing poverty indices, aging population and record-breaking national debt, these security bills, if passed, will likely lead to greater insecurity just at the time when Japan itself is seeking to become a bigger player again on the world stage. Before Abe flexes his military muscles, indulges himself in historical revisionism and preaches to China about the rule of law, he should observe the principle of rule of law at home.

By turning a blind eye on Abe's arrogance of power moment, the U.S. risks not only aggravating the regional tension and rivalry in

Asia-Pacific, but also antagonizing the Japanese public, who came to embrace the postwar values of constitutionalism, democracy and peace.

The Japan Times, July 17, 2015
(Koichi Nakano and Nancy Snow)

TURNING JAPAN'S UNIVERSITIES INTO GENUINE GLOBAL PLAYERS

The balance of power between Japan and China has tilted in favor of China. I'm not talking about disputed islands in the South China Sea but rather inside the minds of the best educated in the Asian region. China now outranks Japan in higher education, according to the recently released Times Higher Education Asia University Rankings 2015. Except for the University of Tokyo that remains the top ranked Asian university, there are now more top ranked universities in China (21) than in Japan (19). China's top two universities are Peking University at No. 4 and Tsinghua University No. 5, ahead of Kyoto University that is ranked No. 9.

I taught at Tsinghua University in Beijing and marveled at the level of English language competence. Students had English names to go along with their Chinese given names and they readily utilized English language media and scholarly journals.

Learning English was seen as a ticket to the world and Tsinghua had its own "English enthusiasts" club that featured old Hollywood movies. I was asked to vote for the best English written essay about "Roman Holiday" starring Audrey Hepburn and Gregory Peck. Not once did I sense that English was viewed as an import language or a threat to Chinese history and culture. It was an enhancer, not a burden, embraced for what it could do to advance the ambitions of the Chinese university students.

Many of those students asked me to write letters of recommendation so that they could attend top ranked American universities. Anything below the top 50 wasn't considered. Needless to say, those students kept me on top of my game in teaching and research. Their scholarly ambition fed my own productivity. I often met with students outside the classroom at a local Starbucks where we would discuss their dreams and career ambitions. It was a lively exchange fueled by a back-and-forth ability to converse in global English.

One day I was returning on my bicycle from teaching a class when a young Chinese woman on her bicycle abruptly stopped me. She asked if I could meet with her to discuss graduate school. Normally I wouldn't advise someone outside of my classroom, but she seemed so eager to meet. When we did, she explained that studying in America was her lifelong dream. A letter of recommendation from me could in her words, "change her life."

When I told her that since she wasn't in any of my classes I personally couldn't write her letter of recommendation, she was devastated. She said that Chinese faculty did not regularly meet with students outside of class or write letters of recommendation, so she was relying on a complete stranger American professor to help.

Despite her disappointment, my meetings with so many Chinese university students helped to illustrate China's global rise in the 21st century. These students who were enrolled at one of China's and Asia's best universities were still hungry for options beyond China's borders. Things that I had taken for granted as a global educator were life-changing events to them. I've never felt so appreciated as an educator.

In contrast, I've taught and guest lectured at dozens of Japanese universities and rarely do I meet a student who asks me about pursuing graduate education overseas. I'm rarely asked anything during a class lecture. In comparison to the Chinese classroom where my graduate students regularly asked me questions, the Japanese classroom is rather silent.

I know all the explanations for this, how Japanese students are prepared for exams and discouraged from questioning the teacher, among other cultural heritage differences. In my many guest lectures I have gotten quite used to the quiet but it still frustrates.

Simply put, if Japan wants to raise its own profile in the world, along with its universities, it must place greater emphasis on group discussion, debate and public presentation.

If globalization were a person, it would be an extrovert skilled in the art of conversation and persuasion, and English (whether second or native language) would be its tool of interpersonal communication.

This globalization "person" skilled in public presentation is not the cultural norm for Japan, a country that historically has been a bit put off by skilled speakers. Japanese studies scholars point out that public speaking and speaking well or skillfully tend to hold more negative than positive connotations. There are proverbs loosely translated as "smart in words, weak in deeds"; "an empty drum thunders loudly"; or "a mewing cat will not catch a mouse." Despite this tendency, Japan can change and it is changing with a more open embrace of the global.

In the last several years there has been a more concerted government-led effort to globalize the Japanese university. Prime Minister Shinzo Abe has called for making 10 Japanese universities qualify among the world's top 100 universities by 2020. It's an unlikely goal, but it doesn't mean that Japan shouldn't aim beyond the stars in globalizing the campus.

I would start with creating an atmosphere that is more welcoming to senior foreign faculty. I retired from a full professorship last year in the United States but have not felt like many Japanese universities would have a place for me.

Several Japanese faculty friends have told me that foreign faculty are sometimes seen as indulged and spoiled in comparison to their Japanese counterparts. Perhaps we are, but that's more of a reflection of the workload of Japanese faculty. Japanese faculty generally teach an overload of courses. In exchange they aren't expected to publish much because there is no promotional payoff to scholarship.

International faculty like myself arrive from a university setting where scholarship is as important as teaching, often more important. It is that scholarship that helps put us and our universities on the global map of recognition. Not only that, but foreign faculty at some of the world's top universities do a lot of media interviews and public speaking at national and international conferences, activities which may be seen as outshining some Japanese faculty counterparts.

Recently a Japanese university expressed interest in hiring me with the proposed title of distinguished professor. This would be a brand new position and the main worry was not salary but how such a new position might impact the wa (harmony) of the campus. Would it incite jealousy among existing faculty?

As long as Japanese universities continue to operate in a zero-sum atmosphere (you win, I lose), then we can expect smaller gains in Japan's global rankings.

Japan's universities can be globally competitive. It will require doing more with less. Right now there are over 700 colleges and universities in Japan, an unsustainable number. Japan will have to close some of the less competitive universities and at least double or triple the number of foreign faculty.

A common myth is that faculty from overseas demand salaries that are double to triple their Japanese counterparts. This myth is based on the supposed excessive salaries for professors in the United States and elsewhere. For the record, my salary as a full professor at a state university was not six figures, but if I taught over the summer and spoke at international conferences it tilted in that direction.

Nevertheless, there is more to being a foreign faculty than just a salary. We global educators who live and work in Japan are here because we want to help internationalize the university. We are not here to be a threat, an imposition, or a spoiled onlooker. Rather, view us as brand ambassadors for globalization and let us help you shine.

The Japan Times, June 16, 2015

BRANDING JAPAN BEYOND ABE

Japan's prime minister has returned from what looks at first blush to have been a very successful personal mission to reinforce to the American audience that "Japan is back," and to remind Americans that Japan stands today, 70 years after the end of World War II, as one of America's closest allies.

As the daughter of a 20-year-old navy ensign who served aboard the USS Missouri eight months after Japan's formal signed surrender aboard the battleship, the close relations between the United States and Japan today are nothing short of a marvel.

Prime Minister Shinzo Abe's congressional speech was designed to humanize a man whose political rhetoric often reflects a militaristic and masculine view of Japan's past. True to form, he began his speech referencing his maternal grandfather, Nobusuke Kishi, who served as Japan's 56th and 57th prime minister. He quoted from Kishi's 1957 speech to the U.S. House of Representatives: "It is because of our strong belief in democratic principles and ideals that Japan associates herself with the free nations of the world."

It must have been particularly exhilarating for Abe to share such a positive memory of his grandfather's post-World War II political career. Abe has been quite open about how revolted he is by those who accuse Kishi of being a Class-A war criminal suspect. The suspicion is legitimate. U.S.-led Allied Occupation forces did arrest Kishi at war's end for his role as director of munitions under Prime Minister Gen. Hideki Tojo, but he was released and never convicted. This led to a political career groomed by those same Occupation forces that needed a conservative anti-communist leader for postwar Japan.

The prime minister has spent a lifetime in dedication to restoring the image and good name of his maternal grandfather. His righteous devotion to the reputation of this one man stands as a psychic block to what is becoming a growing problem for Japan's full nation brand campaign—an inability to get beyond the politics and policies of Shinzo Abe.

Abe does not seem to have the will or the way to devote the same energy to Japan's overall reputation in the Asia-Pacific region and the world as a nation of 127 million can and should do.

If I were to publish a book today on this condition, I'd call it, "Brand Japan: A Government in Need of a Nation." The people of Japan need to be reminded of their value beyond Tokyo's central government, its dominant party, the Liberal Democratic Party, and its main leader, Abe.

We hear so much from the Abe administration about collective self-defense and the need to revise Japan's peace Constitution. Japanese citizens need to strengthen their collective self-defense of free speech and free press. A democracy anywhere, but especially here in Japan, thrives only when multiple voices are heard, when dissent is allowed, and when citizens feel free to express their thoughts and views without fear or favor.

A growing chorus of global voices who care deeply about Japan is genuinely concerned with the Japanese government's hardening of its political arteries. These friends of Japan worry that not only Japan's image but also its reputation is becoming one that is less open and free in its democratic principles. On the heels of Abe's trip to America, nearly 200 leading Japan studies scholars from inside and outside Japan released an open letter urging the prime minister to fully acknowledge Japan's role in the comfort women system of World War II.

The open letter to Abe is a symbolic gesture. While I believe in the power of sincere apology and forgiveness, I do not believe that the prime minister alone can repair the bad feelings in this region. Whatever Abe says, he will be met with a lot of negative pushback. It's a no-win for him. If an apology on his part were met with a grass-roots effort to bring more people into the 70th anniversary conversation, then it might have some positive impact.

While we wait for August to arrive, the citizens of Japan need to elevate the national conversation beyond Abe and any statements he may or may not make about Japan's past. Japan seems trapped in a political straightjacket. Its outward gestures to the world are becoming dominated by headlines reporting the comings and goings and rhetoric of politicians who look largely to the past in order to heal personal wounds or pursue vendettas.

Abe labeled his speech to Congress "Toward an Alliance of Hope" in reference to strengthening U.S.-Japan relations, particularly in collective security and trade.

He notably did not quote his father, Shintaro Abe, for whom my Abe Fellowship is named. Shinzo Abe went along on at least 20 diplomatic trips with his father, who was Japan's longest serving foreign minister. Nearly 25 years after Shintaro Abe's death, the Abe Fellowships support his legacy through sponsoring policy-relevant research that will strengthen the level of intellectual cooperation between U.S.- and Japan-based academics.

Shinzo Abe has also been silent about his paternal grandfather, Kan Abe. This grandfather ran in 1942 as a liberal independent with no political party backing to challenge Tojo's policies, and succeeded in winning a seat in the Lower House. If we define hope as a desire for something to happen, Kan Abe went beyond hope to courage in action in this country's darkest hours. I'd like to see the prime minister widen his reference list when talking about his personal and Japan's history.

In the spirit and memory of Shintaro Abe's dedication to dialogue in international relations and Kan Abe's political backbone when all others were falling in tow with the military line, my hope is for a citizen alliance that moves us beyond narrow politics.

The Japan Times, May 14, 2015

JAPAN'S 'BRAND' AS GOOD

AS THE PEOPLE BEHIND IT

Public diplomacy, otherwise known as nation branding, has never been more important in post-3/11 Japan.

Japan is playing a game of catch up with its recent announcement of the Japan Brand Fund "to fund and support business activities to cultivate overseas demand for Japan's attractive products and services that make full use of the unique characteristics of Japan's culture and lifestyle."

Most every nation now has a public diplomacy entity to promote its unique qualities so even Cool Japan and J-Pop have a lot of global competition.

The winning bid for the 2020 Olympics should put everyone on notice that nation branding is a concern for every Japanese citizen, not just government ministries or businesses pushing their products and services overseas.

A recent op-ed at *U.S. News and World Report* bemoaned the demise of the United States Information Agency (USIA), my former employer, which was for 46 years the official government entity designed to "tell America's story to the world."

Fourteen years ago this month, USIA was abolished as an independent foreign affairs agency. Many in America wax nostalgic for the demise of such a public diplomacy agency, but I don't. Public diplomacy today is not defined by one agency. It involves people-to-people contact, some formal, much of it informal.

A tweet that disparages a nation of people can have as much negative impact as a political leader's statement, perhaps even more since it is so instantaneous and often impulsive in tone.

A personal visit by Lady Gaga to Tokyo after 3/11 garnered as much media attention as a head of state. We may not think of Facebook and Twitter verse in a public diplomacy context, but we should.

More people are engaged now in international battles of narratives and most of the battle is taking place online. The nations that will win will have better stories that inform at a minimum and influence at a maximum, but the people must be fully marshaled in this effort.

Call it an information and image engagement for all.

What Japan should do beyond the Japan Brand Fund is to engage the citizens of Japan in a seven-year path of public diplomacy leading up to the 2020 Olympics. There is no reason that Japan cannot have the greatest show of its cultural history and hospitality that the world has ever seen. If the people from the grassroots up aren't fully invested in Japan's nation brand, then it will show.

This is not just about finding volunteers to serve from July 24 to Aug. 9, 2020, during the summer Olympics. The Japanese government must educate and engage its people about the value of nation branding and call on the people of Japan to work toward the greater good that is the nation's unveiling of itself to the world in 2020.

Of course it is about helping Japan's economy improve, but it is more about showing the world who you are: People before profits.

It is hard to think so far ahead. Seven years is a long time. I've learned from the Native American philosophy that there is always a need for seven-generation thinking. But 2020 isn't even a generation away. It will be here before you know it. And I would encourage everyone to get behind the people's brand that is Japan.

A nation brand—which is just a country's good name and reputation in the world—is only as good as the people behind it.

Don't leave the branding up to a few. Remember, we all are public diplomats in an age of globalization.

The Japan Times, October 10, 2013

PART III.
THE BATTLE FOR
A STRATEGIC
NARRATIVE

HOW JAPAN CAN BETTER TELL ITS STORY TO THE WORLD

As I saw at this year's G7 Summit in Ise-Shima, Japan is capable of projecting a global reality that the world has come to expect: leading-edge high tech, from the world's fastest and safest trains to robotics, electronics and, my personal hope, free WiFi everywhere. Combine this with 21st century high touch – *omotenashi* (hospitality) safety, polite society, humility, modesty, and a green, sustainable economy – and you will really get the world enraptured by your stories, Japan.

The following is a modest proposal for improving Japan's storytelling in the world:

First, Japan needs to get beyond Abe in telling Japan's story. The danger of attaching one's star to a politician is the obvious: the politician will leave office at some point and before that will introduce policies that are designed to divide both home-grown and global populations. Abe has, to his credit, drawn a lot more interest to Japan, but he's also a divisive politician, policy-wise, with many critics arguing that he is taking the country in a far-right ultranationalist direction. It's far more effective to tell a multitude of stories about Japan from the grassroots and the streets up to the suites.

Japan needs to utilize its foreign talent for circumstances far beyond entertainment or business purposes. I often compare my experience teaching at Tsinghua University in China right before the Beijing Olympics to teaching in Japan. In China I was tapped from day one for my expertise in media relations to give lectures to state government officials. I was off campus as much as I was on campus. This was a strategic investment on the part of the Chinese government, which well knows how to tap its third party public intellectuals. Japan does not do that well or enough.

Japan needs to establish a spokespeople and speakers' bureau. I know many talented speakers, but there just aren't enough and there aren't enough women. A related challenge in Japan is finding its own bilingual and charismatic spokespeople at the very top of government and industry. My Keio University professor friend, Tomohiko Taniguchi, has written speeches for Prime Minister and Mrs. Abe. He has a reputation for accessibility with the international press. He is very knowledgeable about Japan's role and function in the world. I would add to this shortlist Noriyuki Shikata, who began tweeting furiously in English and Japanese during his stint as media spokesman for the Japanese government right after 3/11. Japan needs to develop more public relations speaking, but this is practically non-existent now in a country that has no formal programs in global public relations and public diplomacy.

The institutions and persons involved in telling Japan's story to the world need to formalize outreach with Tokyo-based embassies. I've long advocated for more dialogue and discussion with diplomats. No matter what country it is, we tend to view diplomats as people coming and going who hole up in their embassy compounds. The ones I've met are very interested in making their temporary homes collaborative learning labs, but they often aren't asked to meet in less formal settings. Japan has a lot of applied learning opportunities on its doorsteps through international observers and informants.

This brings me to a personally relevant point, especially now that I'm teaching again in Japan as Professor of Public Diplomacy. Japan needs to make its universities more globally relevant. As an educator with nearly a quarter of century of university-level teaching, I have guest lectured at over a dozen universities in Japan from the regional to the nationally ranked like Waseda and Keio. Simply put, Japan does not lead in global higher education. I was proud to be associated with Keio University as a visiting professor but when I traveled or returned home to the United States, very few, if any, have ever heard about Keio University or its esteemed founder, Yukichi Fukuzawa, whose face graces the ¥10,000 note. Japan needs an influx of more foreign faculty with international reputations–it is less than five percent now–and it needs more Japanese faculty who are engaged in scholarship and research collaboration with the world's best universities. How can it do that? Allow some faculty to be research-intensive faculty and let others be teaching-intensive faculty. Too many of my Japanese faculty friends are teaching six to eight classes a semester and they don't have time to do research, much less travel to international conferences. It wasn't until the last decade or so that Japan had to even care that much how its universities ranked internationally, but now with the presence of China and South Korea on the global education stage, Japan is feeling the pressure to maintain rank and reputation.

Japan needs to fully embrace global English and mandatory study abroad. I'm all for learning multiple languages, but I'm particularly outspoken about learning English as a second language. Even if you wish to learn Chinese, Spanish, French, Arabic, Hebrew, Portuguese, or Korean, make English your go to second language. The reality is that global English (and I do not just call it English) is the language of business, diplomacy, travel, the Internet, and most scholarship. While English is readily used or is official in over one third of all the countries of the world (65), it is not even the official language of my home country, the United States of America. I taught to a one-third native Spanish-speaking community of students at California State University, Fullerton. My German study in high school and college resulted helped secure a yearlong Fulbright scholarship to the Federal Republic of Germany, so I've had a bonus in being bilingual. But what I've discovered from much travel and conversation with people around the world is that English is the language tool we have most in common. It's useful, it is fun to learn, and you do not have to be perfect in English to be understood.

I always tell my Japanese students how much I love Japan. Then I tell them to leave this country I love. Japanese high school and university students need to get off the rock and see the world. Once they leave, they will have a revelation. If they are like I was when I first went overseas at age 20, you become more naturally curious. You start asking more questions. You gravitate toward the unknown. Your life becomes more colorful. Over time, you start to relate global travel with having a competitive edge in your lifelong employment, but fundamentally your life will change for the better. You'll become more interested in global matters, and, in turn, become more interesting to a larger pool of people. Getting outside one's comfort pockets in food, language and family is a maturation process that has no substitute.

Part of Japan's story to the world is not just a rising red sun. It's also green. Japan's problems are the canary in the coalmine for the world. Japan's story is enhanced through sustainability and green economy high-tech, high-touch ventures. Japan will probably never become a nuclear-free zone, but the hard-working brainpower I've found here can surely come up with some renewable energy sources that could benefit the world. In that spirit, let's make nature-loving, season-loving Japan beautiful again and preserve more of its history.

Japan needs to release women from their second class status and see how they fly. Unleash women to be social change and business innovation leaders. Women should not just mirror their overtired, overworked male counterparts. Let's encourage women to start their own businesses in social entrepreneurship ventures, where women particularly shine. At present Japan remains less of a start-up but more of a top-down nation where salary workers shrink from leaving predictable work environments. The Japanese value of perseverance in the face of fear of failure must be modeled more, especially for women who, given their second class status, can take risks because they are seen as more dispensable in traditional work settings.

For men and women, Japan needs an awakening of consciousness about civil society, that place wedged between industry and government.

In 1998 I released the first edition of my first book, *Propaganda, Inc.: Selling America's Culture to the World*. Both it and *Information War* were later translated into Japanese. My aim in these books was to awaken a critical consciousness about what was happening in media and government. By then I was a few years into full-time teaching as a political science professor at a small liberal arts college in Henniker, New Hampshire. Along with my teaching gig I held a part-time position as Executive Director and Media Spokesperson for Common Cause of New Hampshire.

Common Cause, whose current chairman of the national governing board is former Clinton Labor Secretary Robert Reich, has a mission that has stood the test of time. Since its founding by Republican John Gardner in 1970, Common Cause has remained a "nonprofit, nonpartisan citizen's lobbying organization promoting open, honest and accountable government." Some of my best material for research and writing in those days came from reports that Common Cause headquarters in Washington produced. Since it is nonpartisan, Common Cause could place issues like lack of transparency or the digital divide into a national context. I didn't have to be too concerned that Common Cause was giving me just the Democratic Party talking points, although nowadays with the rightist turn in American government, I'm sure there are more Democrats and registered Independents among Common Cause members than Republicans. The Common Cause motto, "holding power accountable," could just as well be my personal motto all these years later.

With the proliferation of public interest organizations in Washington, Common Cause doesn't have the punch it once had. After I moved to southern California in 2000, the New Hampshire state office closed due to declining membership. Our member volunteers were skewed to the senior citizens who had joined Common Cause in the 1970s. Young people were joining newer organizations or blogging on their own about pet causes. Nevertheless, as Common Cause New Hampshire media spokesperson, I learned how to address local, national and sometimes international reporters who were covering the comings and goings of wannabe presidential candidates in the state that hosts the first-in-the-nation presidential primary.

There is nothing like a Common Cause organization in Japan. There is no comparable national citizens' lobby anywhere in Japan because lobbying in general is a much newer concept in Japan and any lobbying that goes on is between industry and government. For example, the much-discussed "nuclear village" in Japan is a cozy relationship between industry and government.[160] The people don't have a lobby on their behalf. Sure, there are opposition parties in Japan, but their opposition is mostly cosmetic. Everyone goes along with calling Japan a democracy because elections are held, but there are no effective opposition parties to the dominant Liberal Democratic Party (LDP), the party created from the ruins of World War II as a conservative, anti-Communist bulwark against a rising China. The Democratic Party of Japan (DPJ) controlled the Diet and the Prime Minister's Office for three years from 2009 to 2012 following LDP Prime Minister Shinzo Abe's abrupt resignation from office a year into his first term. But the DPJ was criticized for its poor handling of 3/11 and its inability to offer any good alternatives to Japan's constant political companion. The DPJ's influence in Japanese politics is like a flying saucer in sky watching: a rare event.

What I say in this book nearly two decades after publishing my first book is not that different. The target is Japan this time, and not the United States, which makes my critique more politically risky. I'm speaking to a society that has no lengthy history in cultural criticism and dissent. Dissenters are seen as troublemakers who upset the smooth functioning of the status quo where everyone knows his place and acts accordingly. Japan will have to decide which way it wants to go—to continue on its path of uniqueness or to embrace a path of pluralism that leaves the door open to win-win resolutions. Is it possible to teach English simultaneously with Japanese? Other Asian countries do it with great success and their native languages do not suffer. Is it possible to teach a global curriculum in the schools? Again, other countries do it, embrace their history for good or bad, and accept that today is not the past.

DEEP DIVING: JAPAN'S SEA NARRATIVE

The longer I live in Japan the more convinced I am that its true heritage—that of a sea people–has yet to be fully told. There are some narrative threads emerging, namely the focus on Ama fishing that was portrayed in a popular NHK television morning program, "Amachan." That show is now being used as part of Japan's public diplomacy storytelling[161] and it's a wonderful tool for exchanging non-threatening information with the region and the world about the essence of this nation of islands.

Ama (sea women) fishing is an occupation of spear fishing or breath-hold free diving that is respectful of the sea. Ama divers avoid overfishing target species to maintain and respect the ocean's bounty. Today, in Japan there are about 2,000 ama divers today, half of whom reside in Ise-Shima. Toba City, Japan has the largest number of ama divers in Japan. Why am I talking about ama in a book about Japan's information war efforts to engage with the world? It is because of what Japan has to offer the world in a global strategic narrative. It can teach us so much if it takes a long look at what it already has to share. Look at the ama as a culture and from that extract what are the most important values and beliefs that Japan would like to share with the world. In ama culture, there are four universal values that reflect Japan's national values:

(1) Cultural Heritage: Women whose diving uses techniques that have largely not changed in over 5,000 years.
(2) Respect for Nature: The ama divers commit to avoid overfishing that will deplete ocean resources.
(3) Community Leadership: The ama divers serve as leaders in their sea village communities, where locals live together and maintain harmonic values of coexistence.
(4) Conservation: The ama divers strive to live in harmony with The Mother Sea and conserve the environment through biodiversity.

The Ama culture is Japan's culture. Share the Ama cultural values with the world and you will attract interest from people who want to live more simply and in harmony with nature and with each other. Our world is full of so much strife, bloodshed, and bombs and bullets for profit. We are teaching our children that the world outside is to be feared because you cannot trust anyone, nations are always going to be in opposing sides, and we should always prepare for war.

There is an alternative and that is what Dr. Takeshi Matsuda, president of Kyoto University of Foreign Studies, describes as a "third way" path to human co-existence, not defined by the old US-Japan security treaty or the collective security path that may spell doom for Japan's peace nation brand. In a speech delivered at the University of Texas, San Antonio, he describes Japan's current path toward greater militarization as the wrong direction for a country that suffered so much in the past due to hyper-militarization and imperialism: "I do believe that there is no more ennobling human aspiration than to choose a path towards human co-existence based on non-militarism."[162]

In its World War II defeat, Japan had to embrace loss and a peaceful, nonviolent path under the occupation and military protection of the United States. It became a powerful economy and in 2016 it need not overturn its peace brand for the sake of some nebulously defined collective security. Japan's full embrace with the world must be one that is based on mutual respect, understanding, and Japanese pacifism. Japan has a seven-decade legacy of pacifism and is a leading nation, along with the U.S., UK, and Germany, in monetary contributions to humanitarian aid that enhance human security.

The Japan I'm experiencing now is trending toward the rightwing conservative orientation and ultra-nationalism is on the rise. China and North Korea are everyday enemies of Japan and people here are naturally driven by a sense of fear and anxiety about what may happen in the region or over disputed small islands. The government of Japan has used fear and public anxiety to promote its version of what Prime Minister Abe calls "proactive pacifism," but despite legitimate fears, the majority of the people of Japan want nonmilitary collective security. A state-sanctioned proactive pacifism could lead Japan into a global war alongside its closest ally, the United States, and as we well know, the U.S. has had a mostly tragic outcome in post-9/11 Iraq and Afghanistan. In June 2016, Reuters reported that the government of Japan was planning to buy up to $40 billion in fighter jets "as Tokyo seeks to bolster its air defenses amid creeping tension with China over disputed maritime borders."[163] Foreign military intervention is not the direction that Japan should go because it will risk losing its global leadership integrity of the past seventy years.

Dr. Matsuda offers a perspective that is the best path to Japan's full strategic embrace with the world:

> We as a nation surrounded by the seas and limited in its resources have all the more reason to seek nonmilitary collective security. We must depend, not on military prowess, but on proactive international collaboration, the kind that prevents the country from suffering isolation and desperate need of resources, as it so happened in the unhinged lead-up to World War II more than 70 years ago, on the other side of the pond.[164]

The motto and mindset of my Japanese academic institution, Kyoto University of Foreign Studies, is *Pax Mundi Per Linguas* (World Peace Through Language), from which I get my academic title. Language connotes communication. Communication, when properly used to inform, inspire, engage, and share, is the most fundamental tool of peace and conflict resolution. In Japan's relationship with the world, it has so much to communicate peacefully—from the five-thousand-year-old values of the ama culture—to today's future city that treasures adapting people and place to the environment. The best Cool Japan campaign is still Green Japan, a concept that I first wrote about before my visit to UiTM (Universiti Teknologi MARA) in Shah Alam, Malaysia in December 2013:

A new public diplomacy in Japan seems to be growing out of the immediate post-3/11 recovery and renewal phase to consider non-zero-sum (i.e., win-win) solutions. One such solution is to unite Cool Japan and Green Japan with a major emphasis on science and engineering in Japan to create alternative energy sources for a post-Fukushima era. With Tokyo 2020 seven years away, Japan could revive the Future City of Tomorrow, a city that has the world's best in public transportation, the world's safest and fastest intercontinental transportation (shinkansen); the best technology and science available for a sustainable environment; a model of how to respond to an aging and low fertility society; and a model for how to serve as an exemplary "bridge nation to Asia." Such an approach would require more public participation and public oversight in Japan than is currently in place.[165]

Malaysians have a special place in their hearts and minds for the Japanese. Their former Prime Minister Dr. Mahathir Mohammed, promoted Japan as a model for the rest of Asia and added "Asian values" as a counter to "Western values." There is a legacy here that can be used in Japan's global green embrace.

Japan is a place that makes you feel like you have to conserve, you have to respect your fellow human being, because we are living in such tight spaces. Most of us are concentrated in the city and we stand in line or stand aboard very crowded trains during rush hour. We cherish our private space, which is why you don't see many people staring at you when you are walking around Tokyo. It's as if we are seeking peace in our personal bubble at the same time we are very aware of the masses. This treasure of solitude in the masses is a message for the growing crowded feeling of the planet. Japan will always be a natural teacher about how to do more with less—whether its towns and villages, people, resources, workers, women in the workplace, but within that attrition is a message of preservation, perseverance, cherishment for life and all it gives to sustain us.

It's time for Japan to raise its soft power profile independently, especially in Northeast Asia, Southeast Asia, and globally. As someone who has spent her career involved in international exchange of persons programs (Fulbright, Department of State,

United States Information Agency) I believe that we need to forge stronger people-to-people ties among the big three in Northeast Asia (China, Korea, Japan) as well as strengthen public diplomacy ties with the Association of Southeast Asian Nations (ASEAN). This will require more global public relations training along with techniques in journalism, public speaking, and collaborative development projects that promote social entrepreneurship. I've got my bets on Asia's youth to help sort out our differences. Young people I've taught in this region, China and Japan in particular, are largely open-minded about cultural differences and seek to know more about how their counterparts in neighboring countries are living, working and studying. We need to bottle this and sell it as an elixir of East Asian regional public diplomacy. The alternative—threats to war, hatred, distrust and despair—is no longer thrivable or survivable.

NOTES

[1] What I call my "Japan and I Tour" follows: 1993 International Youth Village; 1994 Japan-America Leadership Exchange Committee; 2010, 2012 US Speaker and Specialist Program, US Embassy Tokyo and U.S. Department of State; 2012 Fulbright Professor at Sophia University; 2013 Visiting Professor at Sophia University; 2013-2015 Social Science Research Council Abe Fellow, financed by the Japan Foundation.

[2] http://www.dropmeanywhere.com

[3] In 2016 *U.S. News and World Report* ranked Clemson University 21st among the highest-ranked national public universities in the United States. The University of California-Berkeley is ranked first.

[4] The oldest of my four brothers was born in 1951. The U.S. Selective Service lotteries for the Vietnam War were held four years from 1969 to 1972. The lottery held on July 1, 1970, was for men born in 1951. All men assigned lottery number between 1 and 125, and who were classified as available for military service, were called to report for possible induction into war service in Vietnam. My oldest brother's lottery number was 204. My second oldest brother was also eligible for Vietnam and his birth year of 1953 made him draft eligible for the lottery held on February 2, 1972. His possible induction would have been in 1973 and no new draft orders were given after 1972.

[5] For a fascinating overview of USIA when it was still an independent foreign affairs agency, see "USIA Overview Brochure," October 1998. http://dosfan.lib.uic.edu/usia/usiahome/overview.pdf.

[6] I was a member of the U.S. delegation from the Youth Programs Division of the United States Information Agency. The International Youth Village was sponsored and administered by the Prime Minister's Office and the National Assembly for Youth Development. It consisted of over 500 participants from 40 countries.

[7] The U.S. Speaker Program is an official public diplomacy initiative that sends over a thousand American experts each year to directly engage with foreign audiences.

[8] *Cosplayer* is short for "costume player," or a person who likes to dress up as his or her favorite comic book character, known in Japan as *manga*, or favorite animation (*anime*) character.

[9] Atsushi Takeda, "Japanese Middle-aged Women and the Hanryu Phenomenon," *electronic journal of contemporary japanese studies* (*ejcjs*), Volume 11, Issue 2, 2011.

[10] "What do you do when you reach the top?," The Economist, November 9, 2011, http://www.economist.com/node/21538104.

[11] National Public Radio, "China Surpasses Japan as No. 2 Economy," August 16, 2010.

[12] Hiroshi Mikitani, Japan is Going English, LinkedIn, July 2, 2015. https://www.linkedin.com/pulse/japan-going-english-hiroshi-mikitani

[13] Ibid.

[14] Kyoko Fujii, personal communication, July 27, 2015.

[15] Hiroshi Mikitani, Japan Needs to Think Like a Global Citizen, LinkedIn, July 8, 2015. https://www.linkedin.com/pulse/japan-world-hiroshi-mikitani

[16] Chris Bruce, "Honda to use English as official language," Autoblog, July 7, 2015, http://www.autoblog.com/2015/07/07/honda-english-official-language/

[17] Government Accountability Office (GAO-06-894), "Department of State: Staffing and Foreign Language Shortfalls Persist Despite Initiatives to Address Gaps," August 2006. http://www.gao.gov/new.items/d06894.pdf

[18] Ibid.

[19] Tokugawa period. 2015. *Encyclopædia Britannica Online*. http://www.britannica.com/event/Tokugawa-period

[20] Ibid.

[21] Martin Fackler, "Japanese Protester Sets Himself on Fire at Train Station in Tokyo," *New York Times*, June 29, 2014.

[22] Article 9 of Japan's Constitution (Chapter II Renunciation of War) reads as follows: Aspiring sincerely to an international peace and order, the Japanese people forever renounce war as a sovereign right of the nation and the threat or use of force as means of settling international disputes. In order to accomplish the aim of the

preceding paragraph, land, sea, and air forces, as well as other war potential, will never be maintained. The right of belligerency of the state will not be recognized.

[23] Martin Fackler, "Japanese Protester Sets Himself on Fire at Train Station in Tokyo," *New York Times*, June 29, 2014.

[24] Jeff Kingston, "Self-immolation Protests PM Abe Overturning Japan's Pacifist Postwar Order," *The Asia-Pacific Journal: Japan Focus*, July 14, 2014.

[25] Ellis S. Kraus, *Broadcasting Politics in Japan: NHK and Television News* (Ithaca, New York: Cornell University Press), 3.

[26] Nancy Snow, "NHK and Japanese Public Diplomacy: Journalistic Boundaries and State Interests," RIPE@2014 Conference: Public Service Media Across Boundaries, Keio University, Tokyo, Japan, August 27-29, 2014.

[27] Anime News Network, "Tv5 To Start Airing Amachan Live-Action Series In Philippines," August 20, 2015.

[28] "Right side up: A powerful if little-reported group claims it can restore the pre-war order," *The Economist*, June 6, 2015.

[29] Debito Arudo, "The costly fallout of tatemae and Japan's culture of deceit," *The Japan Times*, November 1, 2011.

[30] Sean Bell, "Selling Japan: How Much is a Nation's Culture Worth?" Pop Matters, February 3, 2014; http://www.popmatters.com/column/178337-selling-japan-how-much-is-a-nations-culture-worth/.

[31] Cool Japan Fund; http://www.cj-fund.co.jp/en/about/message.html.

[32] Tak Umezawa, "Column: My Cool Japan," Cool Japan Fund, April 8, 2015, http://www.cj-fund.co.jp/en/news/column/5.html.

[33] Christine Reiko Yano, *Pink Globalization: Hello Kitty's Trek Across the Pacific* (Durham, NC: Duke University Press, 2013).

[34] Nobuhiro Ikeda, "Omotenashi: Japanese hospitality as the Global Standard," in *Management of Service Businesses in Japan*, Yasuhiro Monden, Noriyuki Imai, Takami Matsuo and Naoya Yamaguchi, eds. (Singapore: World Scientific Publishing, 2013.)

[35] Philip Brasor, "Tourists may not warm to Japan's welcome," *The Japan Times*, October 4, 2014.

[36] https://www.youtube.com/watch?v=MG_k7dmt0FQ

[37] "Japan, Inc.: Winning the Most Important Battle," *Time*, May 10, 1971
Vol. 97 Issue 19, p. 94.

[38] Nancy Snow, "The Bit and Bricks of Japan's Soft Diplomacy," *The Journal* (American Chamber of Commerce in Japan), June 2015, https://journal.accj.or.jp/the-bits-and-bricks-of-soft-diplomacy/.

[39] Yoshio Sugimoto, *An Introduction to Japanese Society*, Third Edition. (New York: Cambridge University Press, 2010), 148-149.

[40] Kenjiro Takahashi, "Young Japanese rank last in self-esteem, future hopes in seven-nation survey, *The Asahi Shimbun*, June 4, 2014.

[41] Anita Rani, host, "No Sex Please, We're Japanese," BBC Two This World documentary, October 2013.

[42] Peter N. Dale, *The Myth of Japanese Uniqueness* (New York: St. Martin's Press, 1986).

[43] Jean-Pierre Lehmann, The China-Japan-Korea Triangle, *The Globalist*, March 1, 2013. http://www.theglobalist.com/the-china-japan-korea-triangle/

[44] "Japan's demography: The incredible shrinking country," *The Economist*, March 25, 2014.
http://www.economist.com/blogs/banyan/2014/03/japans-demography.

[45] Anita Rani, "The Japanese men who prefer virtual girlfriends to sex," BBC News Magazine, October 24, 2013.
http://www.bbc.com/news/magazine-24614830.

[46] "No Sex Please, We're British," by Anthony Marriott and Alistair Foot. (New York: Samuel French, 1973).

[47] Abigail Haworth, "Why have young people in Japan stopped having sex?" *The Guardian*, October 20, 2013.
http://www.theguardian.com/world/2013/oct/20/young-people-japan-stopped-having-sex

[48] Charlotte Alter, "Japan's Hottest New Sex Trend Is Not Having Sex: Everybody's (not) doing it," *Time*, October 22, 2013.
http://newsfeed.time.com/2013/10/22/japans-hottest-new-sex-trend-is-not-having-sex/

[49] Katy Waldman, "Young People in Japan Have Given Up on Sex," *Slate*, October 22, 2013.

[50] Joshua Keating, "No, Japanese People Haven't Given Up on Sex," *Slate*, October 23, 2015.

[51] Max Fisher, "Japan's sexual apathy is endangering the global economy," *The Washington Post*, October 22, 2013.

[52] Know More from Wonkblog, "Don't worry. The Japanese are having plenty of sex," The Washington Post, October 23, 2013.

[53] 'Greying Japan: The downturn," *The Economist*, January 5, 2006. http://www.economist.com/node/5356731

[54] Richard Hendy, "Yubari, Japan: A city learns how to die," *The Guardian*, August 15, 2014. http://www.theguardian.com/cities/2014/aug/15/yubari-japan-city-learns-die-lost-population-detroit

[55] "Love Plus Marriage," W. David Marx, CNN Travel, November 26, 2009.

[56] "My girlfriend is virtual: An American's experience with 'LovePlus,'" CNN Geek Out, December 9, 2011. http://geekout.blogs.cnn.com/2011/12/09/my-girlfriend-is-virtual-an-americans-experience-with-loveplus/

[57] "Man arrested for placing condom full of semen in high school girl's bag," *Japan Today*, July 6, 2016.

[58] 2014 Global Gender Gap Report. http://reports.weforum.org/global-gender-gap-report-2014/

[59] Global Gender Gap Report, World Economic Forum. Global Gender Gap Index 2015. The highest possible score is 1 (equality) and the lowest possible score is 0 (inequality). Iceland, ranked #1, has a score of 0.881; Japan, ranked #101, has a score of 0.670.

[60] Other documents about Japan's history are far less known but just as revealing about a perceived racial superiority among Japanese in Asia proper and even worldwide. During World War II, the Ministry of Health and Welfare's Population Problems Research Center published several hundred copies of a six volume, three thousand page series, "An Investigation of Global Policy with the Yamato Race as Nucleus." The volumes were released on July 1, 1943 to give rationale to Japan's military expansion policies. A portion of the

series was rediscovered in the 1980s. See John W. Dower (1986), *War Without Mercy* (New York: Pantheon Books), 262–290.

[61] David Barboza, "China Passes Japan to Become No. 2 Economy," *New York Times*, August 15, 2010.

[62] US Reaches Major Milestone: 100,000 American Students Study in China, July 10, 2014. 100K Strong joins Secretary John Kerry and Vice Premier Liu Yandong at the fifth Annual US-China Consultation on People-to-People Exchange in Beijing for Landmark Announcement, http://100kstrong.org/2014/07/11/us-reaches-major-milestone-100000-american-students-study-in-china/.

[63] While my preference is for a full engagement of the people involved in public diplomacy and global public relations, I'm reasonable enough to know that one cannot count on everyone being interested, much less involved, in international relations. It is not something that I would ever want to enforce.

[64] Jerry H. Bentley, Herbert F. Ziegler, and Heather E. Streets-Salter, *Traditions & Encounters Volume 2 from 1500 to the Present*, Sixth Edition (New York: McGraw-Hill, 2015), 874-875.

[65] US-Japan Tomodachi Initiative grew out of the highly successful Operation Tomodachi U.S. military rescue and rebuild response to 3/11. http://usjapantomodachi.org/

[66] The Japan Student Services Organization (JASSO) provides international student numbers in Japan.

[67] Ken Moritsugu and Mari Yamaguchi, "No new WWII apology from Japanese leader Abe; China critical," Associated Press, August 14, 2015.

[68] Foreign Ministry Spokesperson Hua Chunying's Remarks On Japanese Prime Minister Shinzo Abe's Statement On The 70th Http://Www.Fmprc.Gov.Cn/Mfa_Eng/Xwfw_665399/S2510_665401/2535_665405/T1288969.Shtml.

[69] Matthew Pennington, "US experts: Abe WWII statement could help Japan-SKorea ties," Associated Press, August 18, 2015. http://news.yahoo.com/us-experts-abe-wwii-statement-could-help-japan-185317565.html

[70] *Wall Street Journal* staff, Full Text, Japanese Prime Minister Shinzo Abe's WWII Statement,

http://blogs.wsj.com/japanrealtime/2015/08/14/full-text-japanese-prime-minister-shinzo-abes-world-war-ii-statement/.

[71] Shannon Tiezzi, "China, South Korea Not Convinced By Abe's Ww2 Anniversary Speech," *The Diplomat*, August 18, 2015.

[72] *Wall Street Journal*, Abe's WWII Statement.

[73] Jake Adelstein And Julie Makinen, "Abe Expresses 'Grief' For War, But Says Japan Can't Apologize Forever," *Los Angeles Times*, August 14, 2015.

[74] Jeff Kingston, "Testy Team Abe Pressures Media in Japan," The Asia-Pacific Journal: Japan Focus, April 16, 2015. Kingston is Director of Asian Studies at Temple University Japan and has authored or edited many books about Japan, most recently *Critical Issues in Contemporary Japan* (Routledge, 2014).

[75] The first wave of feminism began in Seneca Falls, New York on July 19, 1848, when women met upstate for a two-day women's rights convention (Seneca Falls Convention), "a convention to discuss the social, civil, and religious condition and rights of woman" that featured Elizabeth Cady Stanton and Lucretia Mott, the latter known for her public oratory.

[76] Michael S. Matthews and Jaime A. Castellano, *Talent Development for English Language Learners: Identifying and Developing Potential* (Waco, TX: Prufrock Press, 2013).

[77] Anthony Kuhn, "Is 'Womenomics' The Answer To Japan's Economic Woes?" National Public Radio, December 3, 2014.

[78] Nancy Snow, "Masako Kuriyama, wife of Japanese Ambassador to U.S.: A Woman of Vision," *Washington International*, 8 (4), Jan/Feb. 1995.

[79] Japan, The Hofstede Centre, http://geert-hofstede.com/japan.html.

[80] See the COMD: Committee Opposed to Militarism and the Draft for a perspective on militarism, http://www.comdsd.org/militarism.htm. See also a leading feminist text in international relations by Cynthia Enloe, *Bananas, Beaches and Bases: Making Feminist Sense of International Politics* (Berkeley: University of California Press), 2014. Originally published in 1989.

[81] Japan, The Hofstede Centre.

[82] Japanese Culture & Etiquette Tips, Asian Business Cards. http://www.asianbusinesscards.com/japanese-culture-tips-japan.html

[83] Tomomi Yamaguchi, "'Gender Free' Feminism in Japan: A Story of Mainstreaming and Backlash," *Feminist Studies*, 40 (3), 2014.

[84] Alexis Dudden and Kozo Mizoguchi, "Abe's Violent Denial: Japan's Prime Minister and the 'Comfort Women,'" *The Asia-Pacific Journal: Japan Focus*, March 2007.

[85] Yumiko Iida, "Abe's child care proposal draws fire from companies: Critics say plan hurts other forms of help," *Japan Times*, May 5, 2013.

[86] Shinzo Abe, "Unleashing the Power of 'Womenomics,'" *Wall Street Journal*, September 25, 2013.

[87] Ibid.

[88] Kathy Matsui, "Womenomics 4.0: Time to Walk the Talk," Goldman Sachs, May 30, 2014, http://www.goldmansachs.com/our-thinking/outlook/womenomics4-folder/womenomics4-time-to-walk-the-talk.pdf.

[89] Yoko Sudo, "Goldman Sachs' Matsui Challenges 'Myths' of Womenomics," *Wall Street Journal*, July 10, 2014. See also Women in Parliaments: World Classification, http://www.ipu.org/wmn-e/classif.htm

[90] Chanlett-Avery and Nelson, 2014, 2.

[91] The Global Gender Gap Report 2015, http://www3.weforum.org/docs/GGGR2015/cover.pdf.

[92] "Gov't lowers numerical goals for promoting women to leadership positions," The Mainichi Japan, December 4, 2015.

[93] Tomoko Otake, "'Womenomics' Push Raises Suspicions For Lack Of Reality," *Japan Times*, June 15, 2014.

[94] Off-Ramped Women May Be The Answer To Japan's Demographic Crisis Finds New Study From The Center For Work-Life Policy, Prweb, Tokyo, Japan, November 11, 2011. http://www.prweb.com/releases/2011/11/prweb8951503.htm.   See also Sylvia Ann Hewlett, Laura Sherbin, Catherine Fredman, Claire Ho, and Karen Sumberg, "Off-Ramps and On-Ramps Japan: Keeping Talented Women on the Road to Success," New York:

Center for Work-Life Policy, study sponsored by Bank of America, Merrill Lynch, Cisco, and Goldman Sachs, 2011.

[95] Elaine Lies, "Japan Lawmaker In Hot Water Over Sexist Remark As Government Embarks On 'Womenomics,'" Reuters, June 23, 2014.

[96] Tomoko Otake, "Japanese women strive to empower themselves," *Japan Times*, March 3, 2013.

[97] Noriko Inuzuka, "Women Researchers at a Glance: Japan," White Paper on Gender Equality (WPGE) 2013, Gender Equality Bureau, Cabinet Office, Ministry of Internal Affairs and Communication, Statistical Topics, No. 80, April 14, 2014, 1-4.

[98] Jeremy Diamond, "Reports: Death Threats Against Amb. Caroline Kennedy in Japan," CNN, March 18, 2015.

[99] Yoshio Sugimoto, *An Introduction to Japanese Society* (New York: Cambridge University Press, 2010), 163.

[100] Mary Jordan, "A First Lady's Secondary Role; Premier's Wife stands behind her man, typifying gender roles in modern Japan," *Washington Post*, April 15, 1996.

[101] Suzannah Ramsdale, "Why are French Women so Damn Cool?" *Marie Claire*, March 13, 2014. http://www.marieclaire.co.uk/blogs/suzannah-ramsdale/543662/why-are-french-women-so-damn-cool-meet-the-16-chicest-french-ladies-ever.html

[102] Roger J. Davies and Osamu Ikeno, *The Japanese Mind* (North Clarendon, VT: Tuttle, 2002).

[103] Edward T. Hall, *Beyond Culture* (New York: Anchor, 1976).

[104] Cole Cameron, personal communication, May 18, 2015.

[105] Linda S. Wojtan, "Rice: It's More Than Food in Japan." Bloomington, IN: National Clearinghouse for United States-Japan Studies, November 1993.

[106] Takashi Mochizuki, "Japan's Fancy Rice Cookers Score Abroad," *Wall Street Journal*, July 25, 2015, http://www.wsj.com/articles/japans-fancy-rice-cookers-score-abroad-1438024891

[107] Mihaly Csikszentmihalyi, *Creativity: The Psychology of Discovery and Invention* (Boston: Reed Business Information, Inc., 1996), 73.

[108] Yoshio Sugimoto, *An Introduction to Japanese Society* (Cambridge: Cambridge University Press, 2010), 15.

[109] Brad Glosserman and Scott A. Snyder, "Shinzo Abe's Excellent Adventure in America," *The National Interest*, May 5, 2015. http://nationalinterest.org/blog/the-buzz/shinzo-abes-excellent-adventure-america-12811.

[110] Michael Auslin, "Japan is America's Willing Ally," *National Review*, May 1, 2015. http://www.nationalreview.com/article/417750/shinzo-abe-japan-americas-willing-ally-michael-auslin.

[111] Ibid.

[112] The White House, US-Japan Joint Vision Statement, April 28, 2015. https://www.whitehouse.gov/the-press-office/2015/04/28/us-japan-joint-vision-statement.

[113] The Japan Foundation website states the following about its global footprint: "The Japan Foundation has a global network consisting of the Tokyo headquarters, the Kyoto Office, two Japanese-language institutes (the Japan Foundation Japanese-Language Institute, Urawa, and the Japan Foundation Japanese-Language Institute, Kansai), and 24 overseas offices in 23 countries (including two Asia Center liaison offices)."

[114] "Foreign visitors to Japan in 2015 reach record 19.734 million," *Japan Today*, January 19, 2016.

[115] Rick Noack, "The future of language," The Washington Post, September 24, 2015, https://www.washingtonpost.com/news/worldviews/wp/2015/09/24/the-future-of-language/.

[116] http://www.genronnpo.net/en/was/archives/5236.html.

[117] Harvard University, Japan's global university benchmark, held a symposium addressing this called "Hope as the *New Normal*: National Recovery Through the *3/11* Disaster," October 28, 2011.

[118] Antoni Slodkowski and Kentaro Hamada, "Tepco can't yet be trusted to restart world's biggest nuclear plant: governor," Reuters, Oct 28, 2013.

[119] Barney Henderson, "Tearful Lady Gaga-san tells world Japan is safe," *Daily Telegraph*, June 23, 2011.

[120] H. Gene Blocker and Christopher L. Starling, *Japanese Philosophy*, (Albany: State University of New York Press, 2001), p. 79.

[121] For a visual representation of this turning point, see MIT Visualizing Cultures' online exhibit called "Black Ships and Samurai: Commodore Perry and the Opening of Japan (1853-1854)," by Professor John Dower, 2010.
http://ocw.mit.edu/ans7870/21f/21f.027/black_ships_and_samurai/bss_essay01.html.

[122] Fukuzawa Yukichi, *An Encouragement of Learning*. Translated by David A. Dilworth. Introduction by Nishikawa Shunsaku. (New York: Columbia University Press, 2012), p. 6.

[123] Ibid., p. xxii.

[124] Andrew Tuck, "Nicely done," *Monocle*, October 2013.
http://monocle.com/monocolumn/2013/nicely-done/

[125] Presentation by Prime Minister Shinzo Abe at the 125th Session of the International Olympic Committee (IOC),
http://japan.kantei.go.jp/96_abe/statement/201309/07ioc_presentation_e.html

[126] "SURVEY: 76% don't believe Fukushima situation 'under control'; Abe support rate steady at 56%, *Asahi Shimbun*, October 7, 2013.
http://ajw.asahi.com/article/behind_news/politics/AJ201310070064

[127] Ben Ascione, "Storm Brews Over Japan's New Security Laws," East Asia Forum, August 2, 2015,
http://www.eastasiaforum.org/2015/08/02/storm-brews-over-japans-new-security-laws/.

[128] Philip Brasor, "Tourists may not warm to Japan's Welcome," *Japan Times*, October 4, 2014. Comments section, GBR48.

[129] Teru Clavel, "Culture, cost and proximity draw Chinese students to Japan," April 22, 2015, *The Japan Times*.

[130] Jennifer Agiesta, "Bush now more popular Than Obama," CNN, June 3, 2015. http://www.cnn.com/2015/06/03/politics/obama-approval-rating-cnn-poll/

[131] "The Editorial Notebook – Sushi at the Harvard Club," Jack Rosenthal, *New York Times*, November 2, 1981.
http://www.nytimes.com/1981/11/02/opinion/the-editorial-notebook-sushi-at-the-harvard-club.html.

[132] Martin J. Manning and Herbert Romerstein, *Historical Dictionary of American Propaganda* (Greenwood, CT: Greenwood Publishing Group, 2004).

[133] http://www.publicdiplomacy.org

[134] Nicholas J. Cull, Nicholas J. "Public Diplomacy: Taxonomies and Histories," *The Annals of the American Academy of Political and Social Science* 616 (1) March 2008: 31-54.

[135] Nicholas J. Cull, "Public Diplomacy: Lessons from the Past," University of Southern California Center on Public Diplomacy. http://uscpublicdiplomacy.org/publications/perspectives/CPDPerspectivesLessons.pdf

[136] Edward R. Murrow, John F. Kennedy's Director of the United States Information Agency (USIA), implored that public diplomacy must be in on the take-offs of policy and not just present at the crash landings.

[137] Foxnews.com, "South Korea reportedly confirms Kim Jong Un's wife gives birth," March 4, 2013. http://www.foxnews.com/world/2013/03/04/south-korea-reportedly-confirms-kim-jong-uns-wife-gives-birth/#ixzz2MdJcSihr

[138] Pew Research Center, "U.S. Image in Pakistan Falls No Further Following bin Laden Killing," Washington, DC: Pew Global Attitudes Project. http://www.pewglobal.org/2011/06/21/u-s-image-in-pakistan-falls-no-further-following-bin-laden-killing/

[139] The Bin Laden killing inside Pakistan on May 2, 2011 played out just as the then Democratic presidential candidate said it might in October 7, 2008. During a debate held at Belmont University in Nashville, Tennessee, a voter asked both Barack Obama and his Republican opponent John McCain if either would pursue Al Qaeda leaders inside Pakistan, a U.S. ally. Obama replied, "If we have Osama bin Laden in our sights and the Pakistani government is unable, or unwilling, to take them out, then I think that we have to act and we will take them out. We will kill bin Laden. We will crush Al Qaeda. That has to be our biggest national-security priority." McCain, who often criticized Obama for his naïveté on foreign-policy matters, characterized the promise as foolish, saying, "I'm not

going to telegraph my punches." As quoted in Nicholas Schmidle, "Getting Bin Laden," *The New Yorker*, August 8, 2011, http://www.newyorker.com/reporting/2011/08/08/110808fa_fact_sc hmidle

[140] John Arquilla, "Three Wars on Terror: Ronald Reagan and the battle for Obama's strategic soul," *Foreign Policy*, September 10, 2012.

[141] Peter Beinart, "Obama Shrinks the War on Terrorism," *Time*, December 7, 2009.

[142] Eric Schmitt and Thom Shanker, "Washington recasts terror war as 'struggle,'"*New York Times*, July 27, 2005.

[143] http://www.whitehouse.gov/blog/inaugural-address

[144] Katharine Q. Seelye, "Debate Wrap," *New York Times*, August 19, 2007.

[145] Remarks by the President in Address to the Nation on the Way Forward in Afghanistan and Pakistan, Eisenhower Hall Theatre, United States Military Academy at West Point, West Point, New York, December 1, 2009, http://www.whitehouse.gov/the-press-office/remarks-president-address-nation-way-forward-afghanistan-and-pakistan

[146] The United States Information Agency (1953-1999), an independent foreign affairs agency founded during the Eisenhower administration, was officially abolished in 1999 but the bulk of its programs remain intact as part of the Undersecretary for Public Diplomacy and Public Affairs at the Department of State.

[147] George W. Bush, Transcript of President Bush's Address, http://edition.cnn.com/2001/ US/09/20/gen.bush.transcript/; Julian Borger, "'War on terror' was a mistake, says Miliband," *The Guardian*, January 4, 2009, http://www.guardian.co.uk/ politics/2009/jan/15/war-on-terror-miliband; "Bush: U.S. Muslims Should Feel Safe," CNN.COM, September 17, 2001, http://articles.cnn.com/2001-09-17/ us/gen.bush.muslim.trans_1_muslims-islamic-quran?_s=PM:US

[148] Tom Carver, "Pentagon plans propaganda war," BBC News, February 20, 2002, http://news.bbc.co.uk/2/hi/americas/1830500.stm

[149] William M. Arkin, "Secret Plan Outlines the Unthinkable," *Los Angeles Times*, March 10, 2002.

[150] National Security Strategy, May 2010, 12, http://www.whitehouse.gov/sites/default/files/rss_viewer/national_se curity_strategy.pdf

[151] Transcript of Obama's speech in Cairo, *New York Times*, http://www.nytimes.com/2009/06/04/us/politics/04obama.text.html? pagewanted=all&_r=0

[152] "Muslim Disappointment: Obama More Popular Abroad Than At Home, Global Image of U.S. Continues to Benefit," Pew Global Attitudes Survey, June 17.2010, http://www.pewglobal.org/2010/06/17/obama-more-popular-abroad-than-at-home/. "In Egypt, America's favorability rating dropped from 27% to 17% – the lowest percentage observed in any of the Pew Global Attitudes surveys conducted in that country since 2006."

[153] Nancy Snow, "U.S. Public Diplomacy: A Tale of Two Who Jumped Ship at State," special report for *Foreign Policy in Focus*, June 1, 2004. Republished at AntiWar (www.antiwar.com) and *Asia Times* (www.atimes.com), http://www.fpif.org/articles/us_public_diplomacy_a_tale_of_two_w ho_jumped_ship_at_state

[154] "Longtime Bush adviser leaving," Associated Press, October 31, 2007.

[155] Bruce Gregory, "Public Diplomacy and National Security: Lessons from the U.S. Experience," *Small Wars Journal*, 2008. http://smallwarsjournal.com/blog/journal/docs-temp/82-gregory.pdf?q=mag/docs-temp/82-gregory.pdf

[156] Jeffrey Goldberg, "Samira Ibrahim 'Refuses to Apologize' For Her Tweets," *The Atlantic*, March 7, 2013. http://www.theatlantic.com/international/archive/2013/03/samira-ibrahim-refuses-to-apologize-for-her-tweets/273835/

[157] "Top 10 Economies in the World 2013 – Which World Economies are a Success?" American Live Wire, December 31, 2012, http://americanlivewire.com/top-10-economies-in-the-world-2013/

[158] Peter Kell, Gillian Vogl, *International Students in the Asia Pacific: Mobility, Risks and Global Optimism* (New York: Springer), 2012.

[159] My own doctoral dissertation lent quantitative and qualitative support for such outcomes, particularly when pre-academic cultural orientation programs are included in exchange program grants. See Nancy Elizabeth Snow, "Fulbright Scholars as Cultural Mediators: An Exploratory Study," American University, 1992.

[160] Jeff Kingston, "Japan's Nuclear Village," *The Asia-Pacific Journal* Volume 10, Issue 37, No. 1, September 10, 2012.

[161] Lou Ventigan, "Japan's popular TV series Amachan premiers October on TV5, http://lemongreenteaph.blogspot.jp/2015/08/japans-popular-tv-series-amachan.html. See also The Philippine Star, "Japan's TV series Amachan on TV5 starting October," September 13, 2015; http://www.philstar.com/entertainment/2015/09/13/1499074/japans-tv-series-amachan-tv5-starting-october.

[162] Takeshi Matsuda, "Drift or Mastery: A Path to Human Coexistence," University of Texas, San Antonio, East Asia Institute, October 1, 2015.

[163] Siva Govindasamy, "Japan plans July fighter jet tender seen worth $40 billion as China tensions simmer," Reuters, June 30, 2016.

[164] Matsuda, "Drift or Mastery: A Path to Human Coexistence."

[165] Nancy Snow, "From Cool Japan to Green Japan: The Challenges of Nation Branding," *Centre for Media and Information Warfare Review*, Issue 5, December 2013.

.

www.ingramcontent.com/pod-product-compliance
Lightning Source LLC
Chambersburg PA
CBHW030440290526
45786CB00001B/376